Alexander Astremsky

STORY-FLASH

Step-by-Step
Technology
of Plot Development

for screenplays,
book or stories

STORY-FLASH.COM

Contents

Copyright

About The Book

An author and scriptwriter Alexander Astremsky offers a systematic approach to the plot development. He suggests you stop "waiting for the inspiration" and use the *Story-Flash* step-by-step technology instead. He invites you to rev up the "engine of your imagination" so that you can come up with exciting stories and design them easily, professionally and without the "throes of creation."

The book includes such chapters as "Story Development," "Episode Plan," "Character Development," "How to Make the Story as Compelling as Possible," "How to Develop a Great Comedy Plot," etc. It includes over 60 various practical exercises, pictures and diagrams illustrating this step-by-step process.

This book also includes the *Story-Flash Game*, which you can play by yourself or with others. It is not just an interesting and entertaining game, it is designed to boost your imagination with inspiration and break down the barriers in your mind that prevent you from creating brilliant stories with ease.

About The Author

Alexander Astremsky is a writer, screenwriter, author of the science fiction series *Intangibleworld,* and an economic novel and board games *Money Rules.* He is also the owner of Astremsky Marketing, a company that  operates in five countries and develops presentation materials and corporate magazines. Alexander is a professional speaker and the author of online articles on plot development read by over 500 thousand people.

What People Are Saying About This Book

Edward Akhramovich,
Executive Producer of the group of companies "Art Nation"

This book is in the "get it, read it, apply it" category. Every aspect of the plot development is covered in detail. You are being fully submerged into the technology and can actually apply the tools offered by the author. It's got a clear style and simple language with no unnecessary and complicated terminology.

The Story-Flash technology is laid out according to the principle of "from small to large" – everything is done in small steps leading to a great result. As a producer I really appreciate this approach. The methodology is well structured. Everything happens in its turn: the first round, the second, the third ... The idea, the characters, the plot, the finished structure. All steps follow one another as if being spooled on a bobbin.

This is a step-by-step instruction and I will be using it myself as it's very practical. I strongly recommend this book to anyone who wants to be a scriptwriter or producer. I also believe that everyone who is in the arts industry should read it.

Mark E. Gould,
Media Technology Entrepreneur,
CEO, Carbion Corp.,
Investment Strategist, Exotech

I've been traveling for much of the past 30 years, working in different ventures in media and technologies. I thus, have many tales to tell.

I recently read Alexander Astremsky's book, "STORY-FLASH, Step-by-Step Technology of Plot Development". Of course, in those 30 years, I've many experiences that could easily become written stories. I've preferred in the past to tell my stories rather than take the time to write them down. I had come to the conclusion that these tales would be like "tears in rain" and would pass away when I would someday fade away myself. It is, to be honest, a somewhat fatalistic decision - perhaps, apathetic - to decide that just the experiencing of something unique and marvelous was enough, due to lack of HOW to properly share it. This book offers true hope at last.

What's been lacking is a simple and direct know-how, an uncomplicated technology of "how-to-do-it." This book IS that realized hope, a true solution for the aspiring writer who loves the flow that follows when his muse is engaged to his good service... and the appreciation and sense of accomplishment once done.

In these pages, the reader will learn a comprehensive technology, which he will also very importantly drill and exercise, to an ability to craft a story with all of its essential elements, whether for a novel, essay or tv/film screenplay.

It is not overlong, easily read, written to the point and comprises easy steps for the new or even the jaded scribe. I commend it heartily to your attention AND most importantly, your use. Because, you see, it contains things you can do, in a sequence of steps, to DO SOMETHING ABOUT IT, if that IT you want to do something about is, to: WRITE BETTER, MORE AND ENJOY IT.

Oksana Todorova, Artist/Author (business books; fantasy), President of the Corporate Media Association

Behind the exterior elegance and ease of a work of art, there are always thousands of hours of painstaking work. However, the path to mastery is much more successful if you have a wise mentor. This book is a caring and inspiring step-by-step guide that will take you to the top as a writer. Like a solid foundation, it will serve as a base for your talent. And who knows, perhaps next year Hollywood will make a movie based on your script and you will be invited to the Academy Awards ceremony.

Anna Palenchuk, Movie Producer, 435 films

This is a wonderful book filled with practical recommendations, techniques and assignments. It will be useful to both novice and seasoned scriptwriters. This book has valuable tips for everyone. At last, we have a very comprehensive guideline on how to create this fundamental element of a successful film. The illustrations and exercises will help you assimilate the material quickly so that you can use it to create a million-dollar plot.

Introduction

If you're reading these lines, it means you want to write and sell scripts, stories or books. You want to create new worlds, communicate your message to the reader, you want your screenplays to see their screen versions.

Nothing can make a writer happier than diving into the creative process, and there is no bigger pleasure than typing the words "The End" upon completing yet another work.

But how easy is it for you to develop a plot for a script or a book?

If you are one of those people (there are few) who can simply "sit down and write," then this book is not for you. But if the number of ideas you have implemented is much less than what you have conceived, then perhaps you are holding the very instrument that will take your writing efficiency and performance to a whole new level, as this book is dedicated to the STORYLINE DEVELOPMENT.

This book can be considered unusual – it's written not for pleasure reading or contemplation, but for *immediate application*. In other words, this book is a manual, a guide. You will get the most out of it if you treat it like a practical tool, rather than a theoretical work.

For starters, let's look at the most common problems that you may encounter if you do not have the plot developing technology:

- *You have a great idea, but somehow you just cannot make it into an exciting story.*
- *Your brainstorming sessions go for hours, and yet you are stuck just the same.*
- *You start writing a script or a book but notice your approach is lacking any system.*
- *Half of the work is already done, you've spent weeks or even months when suddenly you realize that "you could do much better" and now you "have to rewrite everything!"*

If you've ever been in those situations, then this book is for you. It describes all the preliminary work you need to do (such as story and character development, the episode plan, etc.), which will enable you to write a script or a book quickly and be 100% satisfied with the final result.

Of course, someone may say, "Why bother with all that? Just start writing." But it's as impractical as building a house without the architectural design: you will spend a lot of time and money, but as a result, your entrance to the basement will be through the attic. At the same time, if you do all the necessary preparations and preliminary work before the construction begins (a detailed design, purchase of the building materials, etc.) a nine-story house will grow by leaps and bounds.

The same approach should be used in the writer's work: preparation and planning come first, then comes the writing.

The plot development technology consists of four main stages:

1. STORY Development. In this step the story itself is created: its main events, characters and conflicts.

2. Creating the Story STRUCTURE. Here all the essential details and events are carefully worked out, the sequence of events is determined.

3. CHARACTER Development (goals, motivation, strengths and weaknesses, etc.).

4. ENHANCEMENT of the Story - increasing the degree of tension in order to "glue" the reader to the book or viewer to the screen.

These four stages form a SYSTEM that allows you to develop the story, characters and plot lines.

I called this system **"Story-Flash,"** which can also be paraphrased as a "story in a flash." It will help you write a screenplay, story or book.

The *Story-Flash* system did not appear out of thin air. It's the result of studying and applying the Hollywood technologies for many years. As I wrote my own screenplays and books, the *Story-Flash* proprietary technology was created and perfected.

Initially I developed this technology while working on a science fiction series *Intangibleworld*. Later I applied it to my book *Money Rules* and in the development of the board game with the same name. When I saw that hundreds of thousands of online users read my *Story-Flash* articles within several months and watched the success of my seminar's attendees, I decided to systematize my know-how and published this very book you are now reading.

Story-Flash is a step-by-step technology. Its purpose is to let your imagination run free, help you develop ideas and devise the plot from A to Z.

How important is this technology to your creativity?

In his bestseller *Story*, the screenwriting guru Robert McKee says, "Of the total creative effort represented in a finished work, 75 percent or more of a writer's labor goes into designing story." This is three-quarters of the author's efforts! The *Story-Flash* technology is specifically dedicated to this part of your creativity. How much value will it have for YOU? Its application will tell.

So, do you want to be able to easily develop plots and stories for great screenplays, books and novels? Let's get to work!

Volume 1. The Story-Flash System

1 STORY Development
This is the step where the story itself is created: its main events, characters and conflicts

2 Creating the STRUCTURE of the Story
Here all the key details and events are carefully worked out, the sequence of events is determined

3 CHARACTER Development
Characters' goals, motivation, strengths and weaknesses, etc.

4 ENHANCEMENT of the Story
Increasing the degree of tension in order to "glue" the reader to the book (or viewer to the screen)

Story-Flash *is a step-by-step technology. Its purpose is to let your imagination run free, help you develop ideas and devise the plot from A to Z.*

Chapter 1. Story Development

The first step of creating any literary work, be it a short story, a novel or a screenplay, is the STORY DEVELOPMENT.

This is the step where you create the story itself: the main events, characters and conflicts.

Of course, first and foremost you should:

a) determine exactly what you are going to write about
b) express your idea in a few sentences

For example, for a while now you've been thinking about writing a screenplay for a fantasy suspense movie *The World of Insects*. Well, write the idea down. It can be as simple as: "The world of the future. Animals are on the verge of extinction. An entertainment corporation comes up with a new type of entertainment called "The World of Insects." Entertainment description: a) a huge abandoned park with countless types of insects; b) participants are shrunk to the size of a little finger so the insects become the size of tigers to them; they are given tiny weapons and sent off to the park to experience the adventure; c) the idea of the entertainment park is to hunt the "giant" insects. The main character, a biologist, gets shrunk and goes off into the park with the insects. However, he is not there to hunt them but to do some biological research. Unexpectedly his tracking device stops working and the corporation employees lose track of him. Will he survive alone in this dangerous, deadly environment?"

After you have done that, you can now move on to the next step, which may take you many hours to complete. But if you do everything correctly, your story will be interesting and profound. This step is called the "Subject Research." By the "subject" here we mean the general content of something.

For example, if we take the idea of survival in "The World of Insects" outlined above, we would research insects, entertainment shows, survival in extreme environments (for example, in the jungle), etc. Research your subject inside and out — read books, study references, research online, watch movies and videos, look at photos — accumulate as much relevant information as possible.

Important: while working on this step, write down ALL the ideas that come to your mind. It may happen that the thought you have written down "just in case" will result in a brilliant plot twist. Therefore, study the chosen subject, write down and keep track of everything that can be somehow useful to you in your further work.

This step can be considered done when you have complete confidence that you are now familiar with the chosen subject and have a full certainty on the "material" you will be using to create your work.

Only at this point, having fully completed the previous actions, we are approaching the most exciting part — THE STORY DEVELOPMENT.

I'd like to note here that the easiest way to see and understand the process of plot development is to take an example of *developing a story for a movie script*. Therefore, we will be working on *The World of Insects* plot to illustrate the use of the ***Story-Flash* System**.

Let's start with some important points you need to know and use when working on any story:

1. Step zero in developing a story – determine what you would like to tell the audience with your screenplay, what it is that you would want to get across. In *The World of Insects* story, we could have the following

message, for example, "Never give way to despair, even if the situation seems completely hopeless."

2. Next: determine the effect you want to create on your audience. For example, to give them a good laugh, cheer them up, inspire or amaze them with the scale of events occurring on the screen, and so on.

3. In the process of creating the story (following the steps below), you should write down everything that comes to your mind. Do not brush any ideas off, it's better to get rid of half of your notes later than to have regrets, "Oh why didn't I write down that idea, it would have come in handy now."

And now I would like to present to you the technology of story development that consists of 21 steps.

After each step there is an example based on *The World of Insects* story.

Steps of Creating The Story

Step 1. Primary Situation

In a few sentences, describe the PRIMARY SITUATION, in which the protagonist has found himself and which he must successfully handle. The primary situation is what the whole story is built around. Imagine that the hero got tangled up in something. This will be the primary situation – the nucleus that will be your starting point.

What is the nucleus of the *Back to the Future* movie, for instance? What is its primary situation? What does Marty McFly get tangled up in? Yes, he goes back in time. But the key question now is how to get back. As you remember, he went there without fuel. He does not have plutonium for the time machine, which means that his chances of getting back to the future are very slim. What happens next? His Mom falls in love with him. Because of that, she cannot fall in love with Marty's Dad, and that means he may not be born at all! Now he needs to not only get back but also keep the marriage of his parents intact. So this is the primary situation around which we start building everything else.

The first step is to concisely formulate the primary situation that has either a conflict, danger or threat – something that the hero got tangled up in. If there's nothing to be tangled in, it's probably not the primary situation. If we say that the primary situation in *Back to the Future* is that the hero went back in time and is doing something over there – that's not it. Do you get the idea? Let's move on.

EXAMPLE: The protagonist (who is a biologist) and his assistant (a lady) go into "The World of Insects" to carry out some dangerous biological research. Suddenly, they realize that they've lost connection with the "real" world and the supporting staff of the corporation — their tracking devices and walkie-talkies are not working. Now they need to handle this situation and get out of there safe and sound.

Step 2. Protagonist

Create the PROTAGONIST. Here is what you need to know at this stage of your work: the character must be created based on his *goals* and *intentions*. We can say a lot about his attitudes and hobbies, but the most important thing right now is the goal he will be pursuing throughout your story.

EXAMPLE: Let's call our protagonist Steve. His main objective in this situation is to remain alive and escape with his assistant from "The World of Insects."

Step 3. Protagonist's Skills

Describe the knowledge, skills and abilities of your protagonist (everything related to his ability to confront the challenges and solve problems). After all, when you have a hero pursuing the goal, there is usually an antihero who will try to stop him. In order to overcome the resistance, the protagonist will need certain knowledge, skills and abilities.

EXAMPLE: Biologist Steve is an expert on insects: their habits, their strengths and weaknesses. He is also very intelligent and can analyze situations quickly.

Step 4. Protagonist's Tools

Give the protagonist some tools that will help him achieve his goals (it can be a device, gadget or weapon). If the hero's skills and abilities are something non-material, then here in Step 4 we are giving him some physical tools. What tool did Marty McFly have in all three parts of the movie? Do you remember his hoverboard? The time machine is also his tool. So come up with something that your protagonist can use for actions in the physical universe.

EXAMPLE: Getting ready for his research trip, Steve takes a detailed reference book on insects with him. The corporation provided him and his assistant with the weapons, tracking devices and portable radios to keep them from getting lost in the park and, of course, the antidote to any possible insect bites.

Step 5. Emotional Wound

As you work on your story, devise the emotional wound for the protagonist: what troubles him, what prevents him from being happy. This makes the character real, complex and relatable for the audience, otherwise, he will remain "raw" and superficial. By the way, if you want to see how this technique makes your script deeper (if you have one in the works), you can give an emotional wound to your hero (if he has none so far). You will be surprised to see this character becoming "three-dimensional" right before your eyes.

EXAMPLE: Steve suspects that his wife is having an affair. He tries to escape the harsh reality by going off into "The World of Insects" and conducting dangerous research.

Step 6. Protagonist's Flaw

Give the protagonist a flaw. This is something that could mess up his plans, something that could jeopardize his victory. You need to make the barriers that the hero is facing hard to overcome. This is what will make the story exciting. A *flaw* is what is going to slow the protagonist down, push him back, not let him win. As an author, you use the hero's flaw to keep the story going. After all, when the goal is reached, the story is over.

And here we can see one of the key features of the "Story-flash" technology at work. This feature is the skillful BALANCE of the hero's opportunities and his "anchors" (what weighs him down). How do we do that? We give the hero abilities and tools that enable him to pursue his goal: the skills that let him move faster, equipment, weapons. But at the same time, we create the emotional wound and the flaw to pull him back down. He is moving forward, and we're pushing him back. The story does not end quickly, it unfolds and evolves! Do you see now how the plots for the soap operas are created?

EXAMPLE: Steve loves insects and discovers that it is difficult for him to kill them, even in self-defense.

Step 7. Antagonist

Now, create the main ANTAGONIST. It's a person (or creature) who will oppose the protagonist. Create him as described in step 2.

Stan Lee, the creator of the legendary Marvel comic-books, says that the nature of conflict moves the story forward much more than its characters. That means that no matter how charismatic, handsome or super-powerful your characters are, if your story doesn't have a strong conflict – it will not move forward. When we create the antagonist, we come very close to the conflict itself. The antihero can be likened to a wall – the protagonist is going forward but runs into the "wall." Moreover, the wall moves towards him and pushes back. The protagonist and antagonist are like two fists that smash into each other. An intense conflict is born, and the story starts evolving.

EXAMPLE: The antagonist in our story is a guy named Michael. He turns out to be the person with whom Steve's wife is having an affair and, unfortunately, he is also one of the owners of "The World of Insects." His mission is to get rid of Steve by any means necessary, but in such a way that his lover (i.e. Steve's wife) does not know about that. He is also the one who arranges for the tracking devices and portable radios to suddenly stop working.

Step 8. Antagonist's Abilities

Endow the antagonist with power. He needs to look invincible, be unpredictable, cunning and talented.

EXAMPLE: Since Michael is one of the owners, he can control all the key staff who determine what happens in "The World of Insects," where Steve and his assistant are trapped. Michael knows all the ins and outs and can directly influence the events occurring in the park.

Step 9. Reason for Confrontation

Describe why the antagonist opposes the protagonist. The main CONFLICT of the script should become very apparent in this step. This is the central tension that will continue to grow and at the end of the movie will burst into flames, putting the protagonist's life and future on the line.

EXAMPLE: Steve's wife (let's call her Mary) is pregnant with Michael's baby, even though she couldn't get pregnant with Steve for many years. Mary hides the affair and the pregnancy from her husband. Her lover Michael already knows about the baby and is very excited. He wants to marry her and does everything he can to make Steve "accidentally" disappear.

Step 10. Antagonist's Evil Deeds

Describe various kinds of problems, obstacles and difficulties that the antagonist could create for the main character. This step is vital, as with its help we can drag our protagonist down, that is, put up some resistance so that he could not reach the goal so fast.

Thinks about it, the events in most soap operas and TV shows could be reduced to a feature-length film. But if your story has the tentacles of various barriers, troubles, problems and difficulties going out in all directions, and there are too many of them, then the story can go on almost ad infinitum.

Once I heard this pearl from Larry Kaplow (the producer of the Dr. House show) at one of his workshops: he said that in order to make the story juicy and exciting, you need to constantly poke the hero with a fork. Poke him all the time. Just keep poking him.

My protagonist from the Rules of Money was very unlucky to be the subject of this "fork principle." Perhaps, that was the reason why my readers asked me time and again, "Alexander, why have you done ALL THAT to him?" The hero of the Rules of Money falls very low to rise high through the use of certain financial principles. At first, I gave him a lot of problems and difficulties and put him in great danger. I needed him to hit bottom to show later how it's possible to turn a bankrupt into a millionaire with the guidance of a financial mentor.

EXAMPLE: Michael can set dangerous insects against Steve intentionally and create natural disasters in the park. He also sends the search party that is looking for Steve in the wrong direction. The search party consists of people with special training who were also shrunk in size. Michael gives instructions to the leader of the search party making them "accidentally" miss Steve and his assistant every time.

Step 11. Secondary Characters

Develop the other characters as described in step 2. They can be divided into protagonist's friends and enemies. Each of them is going to make a difference in some way. By definition, friends help the hero achieve his objectives while the enemies interfere.

EXAMPLE: Mary, Steve's wife and Michael's lover. After Steve disappeared, her goal is to find him and confess. After that she will be able to marry Michael with a clear conscience. Steve's assistant, Julia. She has been in love with Steve for a long time, but she's been hiding her feelings as she did not want to break up the family. While in "The World of Insects," Steve tells her what's really been going on in his family. Julia decides that she will make Steve happy no matter what. Her goals are to obtain the antibodies to cure her daughter of a fatal illness, escape from "The World of Insects," and marry Steve.

Step 12. Three Parts of the Story

EACH STORY HAS THREE PARTS: the beginning, the middle part and the end. After completing all the previous steps, you can describe each part of the script in a few sentences. In this step it is especially important to decide on the ending. Knowing exactly what the end of the story is going to be is one of the secrets to developing the WHOLE story effectively.

EXAMPLE:

Beginning: Steve and Mary's family life is quite dull and isn't likely to improve. Steve is withdrawn and spends most of his time in the lab devoting himself fully to the scientific research. Mary has not been interested in Steve's life for a long time; his job irritates her. She starts an affair with Michael, the owner of "The World of Insects" park. He is rich and gives her seemingly everything that can make a woman happy. Steve suspects that his wife is having an affair, but he does not want to confront her. After yet another fight with his wife, Steve goes to the lab and learns from his assistant Julia that her daughter is sick with a new deadly type of flu. The only hope to save her is to get specific antibodies from a rare insect that can be found in "The World of Insects." Julia tells Steve that she is going to that dangerous place alone. Steve decides to join her.

Middle Part: At some point when Steve and Julia are in the park, their trackers and radios suddenly stop working. They get attacked by dangerous insects, but they have no way of communicating with the park staff. Steve's wife is concerned that her husband disappeared and asks Michael to take on his search personally. Mary knows that she is going to have Michael's baby and decides to get a divorce and then marry Michael. However, she wants to do it only after she finds her husband and asks for his forgiveness. Meanwhile, Steve and Julia fight the insects for their lives.

When the rescue party fails to find Steve and Julia, Mary decides to go into "The World of Insects" and search for Steve herself. Michael joins her as he doesn't want her to go alone.

33

Mary is worried, and she asks Michael a lot of questions about Steve's disappearance. Suddenly Mary sees the other side of her lover: her questions annoy him, and he shows callousness by urging Mary to stop looking for Steve. She begins to doubt her choice. Meanwhile, the search for the antibodies and fights with insects bring Steve and Julia very close, and they realize that they are made for each other. Finally, Michael and Mary find them.

End: Michael fights Steve and tries to kill him. Mary understands why Steve's and Julia's tracking devices stopped working. All the characters get attacked by the insects that were previously released by Michael to kill Steve. Julia is bitten, she is dying. There is no more antidote left as they've used it up earlier. Suddenly, a poisonous insect bites Michael as well. Mary gets captured by another insect and realizes that these are the last seconds of her life. Seeing that Steve is torn between her and dying Julia, she throws him her antidote and asks for forgiveness before she dies. Steve gives Julia the antidote and saves her. The rescue party arrives. Steve and Julia leave "The World of Insects" with the antibodies just in time to save the life of Julia's daughter.

Step 13. Secondary Conflicts

In step 9 we've examined the main conflict of the story. Now think of a few minor conflicts.

I'll give you a valuable tip. If you want to create a book or a script with lots of drama and emotions – create conflicts among the allies. I recommend you highlight this concept if you mark important points relating to the technology. A true drama is built around conflicts of allies (or former allies), not just enemies.

Have you seen The Social Network? It's an excellent film and a great example of screenwriting. You can notice that there is conflict after conflict. Not a minute without conflict! And it's those conflicts (among allies as well as enemies) that create involvement and excitement.

EXAMPLE: In the beginning of the story Mary has a conflict with Steve. At the end she has a conflict with Michael. Steve and Julia are in constant confrontation with insects. You can also show the conflicts within the search party when their leader (being directed by Michael) bypasses their search target deliberately while the other team members suspect there is something fishy about it.

Step 14. Antipathy towards the Antagonist

Think of several ways to make the audience dislike the antagonist: how he should act and what he has to do for that to happen.

The epic show Game of Thrones thoroughly explores the subject of justice and injustice. And it's not a coincidence. If you want the reader to be ecstatic about your work – make sure to right a wrong in full.

And here is the rule: to bring justice, first you need to show how unjust your antagonist is. Create various kinds of injustice, but never take pity on the characters! That's the way to create the antagonism towards the evil in your story.

So, first you created the antihero, his goals and intentions, his allies and helpers, and now let's make it CREDIBLE: create the dislike for him by showing how unfair he is to the hero and the environment.

EXAMPLE: Michael hides the truth about what happened to Steve from Mary. He bribes the leader of the search party and puts Steve and Julia in harm's way by creating natural disasters in the park.

Step 15. Punishment for the Antagonist

Describe how you will punish the antagonist at the end of the story. The punishment must be powerful enough to make the audience rejoice when it happens. The better you do the previous step (make the audience dislike him), the happier your viewers will be.

EXAMPLE: A dangerous insect that Michael released to get rid of Steve will unexpectedly eat Michael.

Step 16. Reward for the Protagonist

Describe how you will reward the protagonist at the end of the movie. What will he receive as a result of his victory?

When creating the ending, we play with two things. The first one is the defeat of the antihero (restoring the justice). And the second is a big win for the protagonist that gives the reader or viewer an explosion of positive emotions and satisfaction from what he has read or seen.

EXAMPLE: Steve will get a wonderful and caring wife. He will collect the research material he has been looking for, thus realizing his life-long dream.

Step 17. Threat

Determine what will happen to the protagonist if he does not reach his goal. This is the threat that is hanging over the main character throughout the story, getting more real and more dangerous with each page.

Athletes have this rule: when you crouch start, turn around and make sure nobody is running behind you with a pole. This is a joke, of course, but you should get the idea that your hero must always have somebody behind him with a pole. There is ALWAYS a threat. Something must continuously urge the protagonist to move forward, and this threat that creates pressure for him will do the trick. In other words, he can't stop and take a break. This is one of the laws of creating tension in the story.

EXAMPLE: The insects that were released by Michael close in on Steve and Julia. Our heroes run out of antidote and their chances of dying increase every minute. They are also followed by the leader of the search party who was bribed by Michael to get rid of them. Steve's and Julia's lives, as well as the life of Julia's daughter, are at stake. Death of our heroes becomes more and more imminent. However, there is something else: if they find the antibodies and the medicine is created, the girl will be saved as well as thousands of other people in the future, thanks to this new medicine. If the antibodies are not found, the epidemic of this new deadly form of flu can claim an unprecedented number of lives.

Step 18. Protagonist's Change

Describe how the protagonist will change. This step may not be necessary for every story or script, but the "hero's change" is one of the secrets to invoking POWERFUL EMOTIONS in your audience and creating a lasting impression from the story. To get some more understanding of this step, recall (or watch) such films as Overboard, Pretty Woman, or the masterpiece of screenwriting – The Holiday, which shows tremendous changes in several characters at once.

EXAMPLE: The change in Steve – he begins facing the difficulties and realizes that at this point everything is up to him. He stops "going with the flow" and tries to take control over the situation, thus demonstrating his courage and strength.

The change in Mary – from a capricious and selfish woman she turns into a person who saves the life of another worthy woman, even at the expense of her own.

Step 19. Secondary Line

Create the secondary line — another (secondary) storyline involving either the protagonist or the antagonist. This is one of the ways to give your story additional depth.

EXAMPLE: The secondary line — Steve and Julia start a relationship. Steve understands that the true relationship between a man and a woman is based on the constant mutual assistance and sincere support in times of need.

Step 20. Mentor

Identify the person from whom the main character can learn something. That is, there should be a person (or a creature) that will help our protagonist use his abilities better and overcome the obstacles more efficiently. In Star Wars we have the Jedi, in The Matrix Neo learns from Morpheus – many stories have mentors.

EXAMPLE: Julia will provide tremendous support to Steve, she will be his inspiration and help him gain new insights.

Step 21. Legend

Create a mysterious and exciting legend (in other words – the background or context). It could be some kind of a myth, something that happened much earlier than the current scene, but without it, the events described in the story would not be as exciting and fascinating. A good, strong LEGEND is one of the main secrets to having the audience completely immersed in the story.

To get a better understanding of what this is all about, analyze the "legend" in such movies as Harry Potter, Star Wars, Transformers, Wanted, The Matrix. All these movies have a legend.

EXAMPLE: At the beginning of the story, before Steve ends up in "The World of Insects," he learns from a reliable source that 15 or so people disappear in "The World of Insects" every year. However, this information is not generally known as they prefer to keep it quiet. What happened to these people? Maybe they got eaten by insects and the corporation doesn't want to advertise that? Or is there more to it than accidental deaths?

The mystery of this legend will be revealed in the second chapter.

In the next chapter you will also learn:

The technology to work out your plot line

The principles of creating episodes and the basics rules for making your plot seamless and integral

By the way, the story of Steve's adventures was created in several hours while writing this chapter to provide you with some good examples. As you can see, this technology really works. See for yourself by following the above steps in the order they are given here.

Write down all your thoughts and ideas sequentially, and in just a couple of hours you will see that the story that could have taken months to "mature" magically comes to life right before your eyes.

Checklist #1. Steps of Creating The Story

STEP 1. In a few sentences, describe the PRIMARY SITUATION, in which the protagonist has found himself and which he must successfully handle.

STEP 2. Create the PROTAGONIST. Here is what you need to know at this stage of your work: the character must be created based on his *goals* and *intentions*.

STEP 3. Describe the knowledge, skills and abilities of your protagonist (everything related to his ability to confront the challenges and solve problems).

STEP 4. Give the protagonist some tools that will help him achieve his goals (it can be a device, gadget or weapon).

STEP 5. Devise the emotional wound for the protagonist.

STEP 6. Give the protagonist a flaw. This is something that could mess up his plans, something that could jeopardize his victory.

STEP 7. Now, create **the main ANTAGONIST**. It's a person (or creature) who will oppose the protagonist. Create him based on his goals and intentions.

STEP 8. Endow the antagonist with power. He needs to look invincible, be unpredictable, cunning and talented.

STEP 9. Describe why the antagonist opposes the protagonist. The main CONFLICT of the script should become very apparent in this step.

STEP 10. Describe various kinds of problems, obstacles and difficulties that the antagonist could create for the main character.

STEP 11. Develop the other characters (him based on their goals and intentions). They can be divided into protagonist's friends and enemies.

STEP 12. EACH STORY HAS THREE PARTS: **the beginning, the middle part and the end.** After completing all the previous steps, you can describe each part of the script in a few sentences.

STEP 13. Think of a few minor conflicts.

STEP 14. Think of several ways to **make the audience dislike the antagonist**.

STEP 15. Describe how you will punish the antagonist at the end of the story.

STEP 16. Describe how you will reward the protagonist at the end of the movie. What will he receive as a result of his victory?

STEP 17. Determine what will happen to the protagonist if he does not reach his goal. This is the threat that is hanging over the main character throughout the story, getting more real and more dangerous with each page.

STEP 18. Describe how the protagonist will change.

STEP 19. Create the secondary line — another (secondary) storyline involving either the protagonist or the antagonist.

STEP 20. Identify the person from whom the main character can learn something.

STEP 21. Create a mysterious and exciting LEGEND (in other words – the background or context). It could be some kind of a myth, something that happened much earlier than the current scene.

Chapter 2. The Episode Plan

The episode plan technology is the main TOOL for plot development.

Any tool is a set of certain ready-made solutions that allow one to do his or her tasks efficiently. Moreover, the difference between the work done with tools and without them is enormous.

Let us take the process of washing clothes as an example. If we lived in the first half of the last century, we would have to do the following: pour some water into a washbasin, soak the laundry, soap it up and leave it there for some time; then we would wash it with a washboard, and finally rinse and wring out the clothes. Depending on the amount of the dirty laundry, it would take one or more hours. We live in the 21st century and instead of the washboard, we use an automatic washing machine, which could be looked at as a fantastic tool that has a set of ready-made solutions. You put the laundry in the washing machine, pour in some laundry detergent, choose an appropriate program and ... the washing machine will take care of the rest automatically. The secret lies in the fact that the washing machine has a PROGRAM – that is, a clear sequence of steps that gives us the anticipated result and saves an immense amount of time and effort.

In this chapter, I am going to give you some ready-made solutions, in other words – a program of actions that will allow you to create the episode plan. However, before delving further into the technology, I am briefly going to go over the theory it is based on.

Let's cover the basics first. Any script can be divided into three parts: the first act, the second and the third, respectively. In the first act we introduce the main conflict (an opposition of two or more forces); in the second act this conflict rapidly evolves (the battle gains momentum); and in the third act the conflict comes to its logical completion (the climax). It sounds rather simple, but we are not here to make things overly complicated.

In the first act we are usually introduced to the protagonist and the main characters, and it also includes the beginning of the main conflict. Here the protagonist finds himself in a certain situation that he proactively tries to resolve right up to the climax of the story, that is until the end of the third act.

The second act is an "obstacle race" for the protagonist and his supporters in the direction of their goal. The obstacles may be so huge that it could be challenging to get around them by plane, forget jumping over them. In addition, even if it is possible to fly over them – there is usually no plane available. In general, the better the screenwriter's imagination, the worse the situation is for the hero because the second act means a lot of problems for the protagonist, and they are getting more and more difficult.

And lastly, the third act. Here, the main conflict gets resolved along with the other minor conflicts. The protagonist either achieves his goal or dies in the attempt. All the questions get answered.

If we divide the finished script into four equal parts, the first act will take the first part, the second act will take the second and the third parts, and the third act will be in the fourth part. In other words, the ratio is usually 1:2:1. However this division is more of a guideline than a strict rule.

And a bit more theory. At the end of the first act there is the first plot point. It gives the storyline a new direction and propels the protagonist into the second act. At the end of the second act there is the second plot point that directs the story to its climax and resolution. These two plot points separate the script into acts. A plot point is always a catalyst for the conflict. It can be a moment when the hero chooses a new course of action, or a noticeable elevation of risk or danger, or an unpredictable move by the antagonist, but it is always an escalation of the conflict and a new direction of the events.

In addition to the major plot points (the first and the second), there are two minor ones – the inciting incident and the main turning point.   Thus, the structure of a professionally-written script looks like this:

1. The Opening
2. Inciting Incident
3. First Plot Point

4. Main Turning Point

5. Second Plot Point

6. Climax

7. Resolution

We will discuss the plot points and other components of the structure in more detail later. The theoretical part is over, and we are now going to tackle the technology.

By the way, after each step you will see an example based on *The World of Insects* story, just like in the previous chapter.

The Episode Plan Technology

Step 0. Describe The Story

After you have done the steps from the previous chapter, describe the story you have developed as fully as you can. All further actions will make it more profound and organized, step by step. Do not worry if you'll have to not only expand but also re-work some events. This is a part of the process that gives your story depth and dimension.

Tip: Don't hold on to something you have written if you can create something better.

Step 1. Create The Exposition

In the first half of the first act we have the "exposition" or, simply put, the opening.

Definition of exposition: an introductory part of a literary or musical piece containing the motifs that will be developed further.

Here you should show the audience the protagonist's life, his environment and his challenges. You need to get the viewer to take a liking to your main character.

This can be achieved by portraying positive traits of the hero through his actions. The actions you can use to introduce the protagonist (and other positive heroes) to your viewers include: saving or helping someone, demonstrating an ability to make their own decisions, ability to control something, professionalism and competence, etc.

EXAMPLE: Steve works in the lab where he studies insects. We see how involved he is in his research and observe his competence in this area. We meet Julia, his assistant. While talking to Steve, she asks whether he is hungry (showing her care) and then talks about going to "The World of Insects" park where they will be able to get all the necessary data for further research. Steve agrees that it would be a solution to their lack of data problem, however he has heard rumors that people occasionally go missing in "The World of Insects." Therefore, he does not want to jeopardize their lives.

Then Steve calls Mary (his wife). We see her at her Michael's house – she is taking a pregnancy test. When Steve asks where she is, Mary says that she is with her girlfriend. The test shows that Mary is pregnant, and she tells Michael about it. He is thrilled and from their conversation we understand that Mary could not have children with Steve, and now she is also happy. However, she does not know what to do and how to tell Steve about it. Michael says rude things about Steve and tells Mary to file for divorce as soon as possible.

Step 2. Create The Inciting Incident

The inciting incident usually concludes the exposition. Approximately 10 percent into the story, the main character must find himself in some sort of a situation that will show the viewer where the whole story is going. The inciting incident creates the impulse that propels the protagonist into another world, a new adventure or some unexpected trouble.

Often this event is the starting point of the main "problem" in the story. It also shows the origin of the "who beats who" battle. It could be a special mission assignment, a discovery of the wife's affair, dismissal from a job and the need to search for a new one, etc.

EXAMPLE: After work, Steve speaks to Mary. She does not tell him about her pregnancy but throws a tantrum instead, "This fly has been buzzing around the room and getting on my nerves for an hour already, but you pretend not to notice it!" Mary says that she is leaving Steve because she is tired of his useless job and that empty life. From their further conversation and certain indicators, Steve realizes that Mary is having an affair. The next day Steve goes to work and learns from Julia that her daughter is terminally ill with a new type of flu. Her only hope is getting the antibodies carried by a rare insect that lives in "The World of Insects." Julia tells Steve that she is going to that dangerous place and Steve decides to go there with her.

Step 3. Work On The Orientation Period

After the exposition and before the first plot point, there is a period when the protagonist gets oriented in the new environment (where he wound up due to the inciting incident). At the same time, we should also orient the AUDIENCE as to where the protagonist is, his surroundings, existing threats in his environment, and what will happen if the evil wins. By "evil" here we mean something that prevents the main character from having a happy life and what stands in the way of achieving his goals.

EXAMPLE: Steve and Julia arrive at "The World of Insects." We learn that it's a huge park with many different insects. The corporation specializes in providing the following entertainment: a person gets shrunk to the size of a little finger (don't forget that this is happening in the future), they give him a special weapon, a first aid kit and everything else he will need to hunt insects. Then he is sent off to the park (as if into the jungle) for a few days. In short, this is one of the most dangerous forms of entertainment in the future. The administrator sends Steve and Julia to see the CEO of the corporation to make arrangements for their research trip. The CEO turns out to be Michael (Mary's lover). Steve and Michael have never met each other before.

With a smile, Michael gives them permission to conduct the research. Steve and Julia get equipped with the hunting gear, shrunk and transported to the park. The adventure begins. Our heroes look around ... Suddenly, a dangerous insect appears out of nowhere and stings Steve. Without hesitation, Julia cold-bloodedly kills the insect with a special weapon and quickly gives Steve the antidote. He recovers, and now it's the time for the first plot point.

Step 4. Develop The First Plot Point

It takes place at the end of the first act, approximately one quarter into the story. This is the transition from the first act into the second. This is a place where something makes the protagonist go along a certain way or pushes him to make a decision that the audience was not expecting. This is the moment when the main character STARTS on the way that should lead him to his goal.

Ideally, the first plot point wipes out any possibilities for the protagonist to return to the same old course of life. This is actually one of the key factors that contributes to the viewer's interest in your story!

To get the idea of how this works, think of the movie Speed. Remember how you just can't look away from the screen from the very moment the antagonist tells the police that the bus must not go slower than 80 km/h? The same goes for The Matrix when Neo chooses the red pill, and for Back to the Future where the hero ends up in the past and has almost no chances of getting back to the present.

You will be able to create the first plot point masterfully if you understand that this event is a powerful impetus for all the action in the second act (i.e. a large number of activities aimed at achieving the hero's goal). Therefore, here you need to set the exact direction for all further developments and events.

EXAMPLE: Steve and Julia discover that their radios and trackers are not working. They cannot contact the outside world, and the "outside world" cannot track their location. They are lost in the depths of the park (just like in the jungle) and have no way of finding their bearings.

Step 5. Work On The Adjustment Period

Between the first plot point and the main turning point, there is an adjustment period. For the next 25 percent (one quarter) of your story, the main character adjusts to the circumstances resulting from the first plot point. He tries to predict the future events, makes plans to achieve his objective and prepares for action.

In this step you also need to describe what the antagonist and (or) his supporters are doing meanwhile.

EXAMPLE: After the first plot point Steve and Julia have a very clear objective — to escape from "The World of Insects." At first, they hope that their tracking devices and radios start working again, but that doesn't happen. Then they start looking for a solution. They analyze their resources: weapons, antidotes, food and water supplies, and so on. They are also happy that they have a reference book with the information on all known insects.

After that our heroes have to defend themselves twice from the insect attacks, and both times Julia is the one who kills them. Steve's weakness becomes obvious — it is hard for him to kill insects. Then Steve and Julia notice a scavenger insect. Since there are absolutely no animals or birds of any kind in the park, it makes our biologists concerned and they start suspecting that something is not right here. They follow this insect and suddenly fall into a strange tunnel. At the bottom of the tunnel they find ... a human skeleton with some clothes remains. Steve picks up the identity card he found near the bones. He tells Julia that it seems to be the body of the politician who went missing in "The World of Insects" last year. Our heroes also see ... a bullet hole in his skull.

At this point we learn that Michael was the one who arranged for the trackers and radios to stop working. Immediately after that, he orders the search party to go look for Steve and Julia. Then he calls Mary and tells her that her husband is missing and that he has already sent the search party to find and save him and his assistant. After that he calls the leader of the search party (John) to his office and orders him to get rid of Steve and Julia by any means. From their conversation we understand that John is "Michael's man" unlike the rest of the team. Therefore, the mission of destroying Steve and his assistant is entirely up to him and it must be done in complete secrecy from the other team members.

Step 6. Develop The Main Turning Point

Approximately in the middle of the story there is the so-called main turning point. This is the moment when the protagonist becomes more of a master of the situation rather than a person who is going with the flow. His chances of winning increase thanks to his new knowledge, skills or abilities. Now he is 100 percent sure that he can reach his goal. Often this is the moment when the hero "burns all the bridges," and the viewers realize that there is no turning back. The motto is "Never look back!"

The key to creating the main turning point professionally is the understanding that from this point on, the protagonist does not just follow the path towards his goal but begins acting very DELIBERATELY in order to reach it.

EXAMPLE: Near the skeleton Steve and Julia find a hunting map and a special navigation device. They were not given either one of those tools because they went there for the research purposes, not hunting; also, the corporation employees were going to get them out of the park in the evening. Now they have something that will help them find their way out. With the help of the device they determine their location and use the map to start moving in the right direction. We can also see how Steve kills another attacking insect himself. That means he has overcome his weakness concerning the insects and now he is a real fighter, bravely attacking the dangers of the park.

Step 7. Work Out The Action Period

Between the main turning point and the second plot point, the main character and his team are proactive and deliberate in their fight with evil. This is the second half of the second act and this part of the script has the most intense action for both positive and negative characters.

Write down the actions of the main character and the members of his team; then describe the dirty deeds of the antagonist and his supporters at this point of the story.

The key to doing this step correctly is the understanding of the principle "every action has an equal and opposite reaction;" in other words, when the protagonist moves forward — the antagonist pushes him back. The size of the goal determines the size of the obstacles and challenges on the way towards it. It is the law of life and the law of creating a great story.

EXAMPLE: Steve and Julia fight giant insects and move towards the park exit. Unexpectedly, they find another tunnel similar to the one where they found the body of the politician. When they look inside, they find ... more bones. Our characters connect the dots and realize that this is the location where contract killings of influential people take place. After all, it is a perfect place for that. Who from the "outside world" will ever be able to find a skeleton of a person who was shrunk to the size of a little finger? But then the mastermind behind these murders must be somebody who has all the bases covered in "The World of Insects"....

Meanwhile, Mary arrives at the corporation. She informs Michael that she decided to tell Steve everything. Only after that she will be able to divorce him with a clear conscience. Michael says that so far there is no news about Steve. Mary begins to suspect that Michael is responsible for Steve's disappearance and they have a fight. Michael gets angry and accuses Mary, "How could she think such a thing?" Mary demands Michael go with her to the park and help her find Steve. Michael agrees. He and Mary get equipped as hunters and are sent off into the park. Right before they leave Michael releases specific insects that are very dangerous. He knows that Steve has no antidote for their poison and hopes that these insects will finish Steve off if he is still alive.

Steve and Julia hunt a quick and elusive insect — the one that carries the antibodies. Finally, they catch it and obtain their "quest object" — the antibodies for the medicine.

The search party finds Steve and Julia's tracks and rushes to their rescue. However, the leader of the search party (John) tries to throw his group off their track and succeeds. One of the team members (Robert) has a disagreement with John and refuses to do what the leader tells him. John dismisses Robert from the team and orders him to get out of the park.

Step 8. Develop The Second Plot Point

Mr. "Second Act" brought a lot of trouble to our protagonist and gave him a really rough time on his way to the goal. But now the main problems are behind him (or so he thinks) and the victory is close ... He has to take just one more step, open the last door, pull the trigger and ... all of a sudden, there is the second plot point. THE PLAN HAS FAILED!!! The smell of victory disappears and gets replaced by the stench of the villain who pins our hero against the wall with all his might. We can call this moment a "big failure." This is the transition to the third act.

The second plot point acts as a catalyst for tension and conflict. It makes the protagonist take the most drastic measures here and now. After all, he did not give up! The goal can still be achieved! Thus, the second plot point puts the protagonist in a situation where he has to make one last decisive effort to win or die in the attack.

EXAMPLE: Steve and Julia are excited that they have almost reached the exit when suddenly terrifying insects start attacking them. During the battle Julia falls into the tunnel, similar to the one where they found the corpses. Steve tries to get her out while fighting off the insects. At that moment John appears near Steve – he has quietly broken away from the search party – and orders Steve to jump into the tunnel. After a short conversation between them, we finally understand that John is the hitman for the contract killings and Michael covers up for him. Suddenly we hear a shot and see John dead – Robert, who followed him and witnessed the conversation, shoots John.

Step 9. Work Out The Protagonist's Crisis

In order to win, you have to look inside yourself and reconsider some of your views or ideas. After all, something has brought the protagonist to failure or gave him big problems (either wrong ideas or his modus operandi). So if he gets to the bottom of his fears, doubts, weaknesses or mistakes ... he can still win. Here is the principle used by wise people striving for their goals, "If my plan has failed, that means something needs to be changed." Most often, it concerns one's own modus operandi or views on life. Hence, here comes the "protagonist's crisis."

This is the biggest test for the hero's character, a review of established principles or return to his lost ideals.

The crisis poses a difficult choice for the main character, and this is the critical moment in the story. This episode shows us whether the protagonist gave up or remained unwavering, whether he started fully believing in himself or could not overcome his weaknesses.

This crisis can happen right before the final battle (see the following step) or even in the middle of it.

EXAMPLE: In our story, the "protagonist crisis" will take place during the final battle. Steve will have to choose between saving the life of either Julia or Mary – both will be dying from the deadly sting and the remaining antidote can save only one of them. Steve will choose Julia as his true soulmate (which he realized during their dangerous adventures).

Step 10. Create The Final Battle

From the second plot point on, the main character will have to give it his all so that despite everything, he can still achieve his goal. The chance of winning is minimal, the risk and conflict are at their highest, and the protagonist enters the final battle with the antagonist.

During the final battle the audience should feel that everything is working against the protagonist and that he is about to lose or die. Often it is the most emotional moment of the story due to the fullest manifestation of good and evil.

By the way, if we show that the protagonist was able to

defeat evil because of his internal change, the viewer can experience a real emotional outburst.

EXAMPLE: Michael and Mary find our heroes. When Michael finds out who shot John, he immediately kills Robert. By this time Steve has already pulled Julia out of the tunnel, however, she is dying in his arms from the sting for which they have no antidote. Mary offers her antidote to Julia and then tells Steve that she is pregnant from Michael. At that moment one of the insects that Michael released to kill Steve attacks her. Michael tries to protect Mary, but the insect stings both of them. He takes out his antidote and injects himself with the whole dose.

Julia has not used Mary's antidote yet. She is dying but offers it to Mary. Mary refuses. Michael snatches the remedy from Julia's hand and starts walking towards Mary. At this moment another insect catches Michael and starts swallowing him.

Step 11. Create The Climax

Definition of the word climax: a point of the highest tension, enthusiasm, development of something.

The final battle ends with the climax. This is the moment of liberation, the triumph of the principles embodied by the main character in his actions. And of course, it is the final victory, everything he fought for so hard right to the very end (this victory, mind you, could have been won at the cost of his own life). The climax occurs between approximately the 90 percent mark of the story and the last several minutes.

EXAMPLE: Steve barely manages to grab the antidote from Michael's hands as he disappears inside the "predator." Steve takes several shots at the insect that swallowed Michael, and it quickly goes out of sight. Then he comes up to Julia and gives her the antidote. He approaches Mary and says goodbye to her with tears in his eyes. Mary dies. Insects retreat. The search party is on its way to our heroes.

Step 12. Describe The Resolution

The resolution is the part of the script located between the climax and the words "The End." Professional creation of resolutions is a true art. It is worth mastering, of course, if you don't want people to say that the endings of your scripts are weak.

Here is what needs to happen after the climax:

1. The main character and (or) those affected by his victory need to understand what it means for them. Give the audience a taste of the win and show the joy!

2. You need to show that the victory is final, and the evil is not likely to return (at least soon).

3. Then show how the life of the protagonist and (or) his team has changed after the evil was defeated.

4. Finally, the resolution's most important point – the demonstration of the hero's ideals that are now a reality.

These four points give the movie a sense of completeness, and the viewer leaves the movie theatre very satisfied.

EXAMPLE (in the same sequence):

1. Steve takes Julia in his arms and they are looking at the approaching search party. Julia looks at the vial with the antibodies in her hand. We can see the calm in her eyes. Then she passes out.

2. The next scene: we see the police and people in uniforms near the bones in the tunnels. Next, we see the main entrance of the corporation, the notice on the office doors reads "Temporarily Closed."

3. Morning. Steve and Julia are sleeping in the same bed.

4. Julia opens her eyes slightly and says to Steve half-

asleep, "Darling, this fly has been buzzing around the room for an hour already. It keeps waking me up." Steve opens his eyes and looks at Julia tensely. She continues, "Shall we catch it? For experiments." Steve smiles. Julia puts her head on his shoulder and he embraces her. Julia's happy daughter knocks on the door and peeks into the room. We see "The End" appear on the screen.

Step 13. Create The Timeline

The timeline is an auxiliary tool that is a MAP of the sequence of events.

By now your story should have taken a complete form, but you may still have some confusion in your thoughts. To handle it, I strongly recommend doing the following:

Take three A4-size sheets of paper and glue them together so that you get a long landscape sheet (3x longer than a standard sheet).

Draw a horizontal line on the paper that goes through all three sheets. This will be the movie's timeline.

Draw seven "flags" or seven vertical bars on this line and mark them as follows: the opening, the inciting event (10 percent from the beginning), the first plot point (25 percent), the main turning point (50 percent), the second plot point (75 percent), the climax (at any point between the 90 and 99 percent) and the end.

Now put the glued sheets vertically so that the flag for the opening is at the top.

Take a pen or a pencil and consecutively describe all the events you have developed by now locating them on the timeline between the flags.

The mathematical accuracy of placing the events is not too significant here; what's important is that you transfer the key points of the story onto the timeline (on the paper, that is).

This is an excellent remedy for the confusion in your head. Try it!

Step 14. Divide The Story Into Episodes

An episode is a series of scenes united by a common location or subject. In other words, an episode consists of scenes, not vice versa.

A scene is a separate part of the action. In our case, it's a part of an episode.

Each episode is a small story that has a beginning, middle part, and the end. For example, if the main character took three minutes to go to the store to get some bread, it can be considered an episode. However, his banter with the saleswoman in the store is a scene (one minute). The moment when he met his classmate Maria on his way back home could be another scene (one minute). So "going out to get bread —

buying bread — coming back" is an episode and the events taking place during his "trip to get the bread" are scenes.

Each episode usually takes about three minutes (but this is not a strict rule). Now, after all the work that you've done, you'll need to divide the story into approximately 40 parts to make the episode plan. The timeline tool will help you see the parts (episodes) that your story consists of.

EXAMPLE:

Episode 1: Steve works in his lab, he is studying insects and talking to Julia. She says that it would be great to get into "The World of Insects" park because there they would be able to obtain all the necessary data for further research and materials for writing the academic paper. However, Steve doesn't like this idea – there are rumors that people occasionally go missing in "The World of Insects" and he does not want to jeopardize Julia's or his life.

Episode 2. Steve calls Mary. She is taking a pregnancy test. Steve asks where she is, and Mary tells him that she is with her girlfriend. The test shows that Mary is pregnant, and she tells Michael about it. He is thrilled and from their conversation we understand that Mary could not have children with Steve, and now she is also happy. However, she does not know what to do and how to tell Steve about it. Michael says rude things about Steve and tells Mary to file for divorce as soon as possible.

Episode 3. After work, Steve speaks to Mary. She does not tell him about her pregnancy but throws a tantrum instead: "This fly has been buzzing around the room and getting on my nerves for an hour already, but you pretend not to notice it!" Mary says that she is leaving Steve because she is tired of his useless job and that empty life. From their further conversation and certain indicators, Steve realizes that Mary is probably having an affair. Mary leaves.

Step 15. Ensure Having The Elements That Advance The Plot

Each episode should actively move the story forward. Therefore, in this step go through all the episodes sequentially and make sure each of them has the elements that advance the plot.

An element that advances the plot is the point that makes the story DEVELOP.

EXAMPLE:
Episode 1. We learn that the only way for Steve to obtain the necessary data for his further research is to go to "The World of Insects."

Episode 2. Michael tells Mary to get a divorce immediately.

Episode 3. Mary leaves Michael.

So if you have described all the episodes, and each of them has an element that moves the plot forward —

congratulations! Your episode plan is ready. And here's one last piece of advice.

Step 16. Make The List Of All Episodes And Name Them

Many people write the to-do lists to increase their productivity (what should be done, plan for the week, etc.). This helps concentrate on the tasks and goals.

Now that your episode plan is done, I recommend you make a list of episodes and give them short titles. This will be your "to-do list." Print it out and hang over your table. When you work on the script, you will move forward according to this list. And believe me, you will experience great satisfaction when you check the item off this plan after you finalize that episode in your SCRIPT.

EXAMPLE:

List of Episodes

1. Steve talks to Julia in the lab
2. Mary finds out she is pregnant
3. Steve and Mary fight
And so on ...

We have now reviewed the last step of the episode plan technology.

You will probably have to use all your mental capacity and abilities to the fullest. Nevertheless, if you learn this tool, you will be able to tackle those ideas that you didn't dare to touch before. More importantly, now you can carefully plan out your script before you start writing so that after you are done, there's no need to keep rewriting it.

We live in the 21st century, and we have tools and ready-made solutions. We deserve great movies, but whether we will have them or not depends on what you are doing today with your screenplay.

STORY-FLASH. The Storyline Structure: 12 Components

Step 1 Story-Flash Structure	Step 2 Story-Flash Structure	Step 3 Story-Flash Structure
THE EXPOSITION	THE INCITING INCIDENT	THE ORIENTATION PERIOD
0-10 %	10 %	10-25 %

Step 4 Story-Flash Structure	Step 5 Story-Flash Structure	Step 6 Story-Flash Structure
THE FIRST PLOT POINT	THE ADJUSTMENT PERIOD	THE MAIN TURNING POINT
25 %	25-50 %	50 %

Step 7 Story-Flash Structure	Step 8 Story-Flash Structure	Step 9 Story-Flash Structure
THE ACTION PERIOD	THE SECOND PLOT POINT	THE PROTAGONIST'S CRISIS
50-75 %	75 %	Between 75-95 %

Step 10 Story-Flash Structure	Step 11 Story-Flash Structure	Step 12 Story-Flash Structure
THE FINAL BATTLE	THE CLIMAX	THE RESOLUTION
Between 75-95 %	End of the final battle	95-100 %

Checklist #2. The Episode Plan Technology

STEP 1. CREATE THE EXPOSITION

STEP 2. CREATE THE INCITING INCIDENT

STEP 3. WORK ON THE ORIENTATION PERIOD

STEP 4. DEVELOP THE FIRST PLOT POINT

STEP 5. WORK ON THE ADJUSTMENT PERIOD

STEP 6. DEVELOP THE MAIN TURNING POINT

STEP 7. WORK OUT THE ACTION PERIOD

STEP 8. DEVELOP THE SECOND PLOT POINT

STEP 9. WORK OUT THE PROTAGONIST'S CRISIS

STEP 10. CREATE THE FINAL BATTLE

STEP 11. CREATE THE CLIMAX

STEP 12. DESCRIBE THE RESOLUTION
IMPORTANT: Here is what needs to happen after the climax:

1. *The main character and (or) those affected by his victory need to understand what it means for them. Give the audience a taste of the win and show the joy!*

2. *You need to show that the victory is final, and the evil is not likely to return (at least soon).*
3. *Then show how the life of the protagonist and (or) his team has changed after the evil was defeated.*
4. *Finally, the resolution's most important point – the demonstration of the hero's ideals that are now a reality.*

STEP 13. CREATE THE TIMELINE

STEP 14. DIVIDE THE STORY INTO EPISODES

STEP 15. ENSURE HAVING THE ELEMENTS THAT ADVANCE THE PLOT

STEP 16. MAKE THE LIST OF ALL EPISODES AND NAME THEM

Chapter 3. Character Development

For many decades one of the main problems of the cinema has been the superficial approach of screenwriters to character development. Some believe that it is not particularly important, others have the characters develop "on their own." Then there are those who simply don't know how to do it correctly.

Try answering the following questions without much consideration:

1. What is the main objective of character development?

2. At which point when you are writing a script is it necessary to start developing the characters?

3. What is the starting point for developing any character?

4. What are the steps of the development process?

Were you able to do that? After all, not knowing the answers to these questions will significantly slow you down in your work, lower the quality of your script, and could bring your story to a dead end.

In this chapter I will try to show that the character development is a separate and exciting stage of scriptwriting, and it is by no means something that just happens somewhere along the line.

Here you will find the CHARACTER DEVELOPMENT TECHNOLOGY that has thirteen consecutive steps. Each step covers a particular stage of that process.

Let's start with the theory and consider the fundamental components of the character development technology.

Theory of Character Development (four key principles)

The first datum is: **a script consists of the STEPS that the CHARACTERS make towards the resolution.** Each step is a certain action or phrase. Steps make up scenes; scenes make up episodes, and episodes make up the finished script. So it's pretty obvious that each character CONTRIBUTES to the events and as a result, we have a finished story.

The second fundamental datum is: **each character has his own FUNCTION that impacts the creation of a finished story.** The word "function" is defined as a duty, range of activities, purpose, role.

Character's function (as well as the reason for having this character in the script) becomes clear when you answer these questions: WHAT and WHY will the character do in the story? Each character must move your story in a certain DIRECTION and advance the plot with his contributions.

Let's look at an example of this in business. A good manager will never hire employees just to make the company look better or brighter. He hires them to do specific jobs that will contribute to the company's success.

We should treat our characters the same way: hire (create) those who are necessary for your story and fire (cut out) the "unnecessary" ones. In a script, just like in business, the work of several people could often be done by a single person.

The third datum of this technology is: **character development is a process that happens concurrently with the creation of the story.** To understand how this happens, let's take a look at the FIVE STAGES OF CREATING ANY STORY.

Stage 1. Goal and Counter Goal

First off, for the story to begin, we need to create a goal for the main character, and then we need to create a counter goal. Now we have the primary situation in which our protagonist finds himself.

The counter goal is a goal that is directed against or opposes the other goal. For example, if Bob wants to date Natalie but Natalie does not want to date Bob, we can say that she has a counter goal (that opposes Bob's goal). Another scenario: Bob wants to date Natalie, but Jack also wants to date Natalie, so here the counter goal (the one opposing Bob's goal) will be Jack's.

Stage 2. Protagonist and Antagonist

Now that we have a clear goal and an opposing counter goal, we create the character who is the best fit for this goal. That is how we get our protagonist – the main character of the story. HE is the one who will face the main problem. He is the one who will work hard to solve it and we will follow him through the whole story until the very end. All the plot lines are built around the protagonist and his GOAL.

Then we create the antagonist who in turn has the counter goal. Who is an antagonist? Most often, it is the second most significant character in the story. If you have already used the technology from the previous chapters, you have probably noticed that the story is created primarily through developing the protagonist and the antagonist. Then the story is built on the conflict of their goals. Therefore, the main thing you should know about the antagonist is that you develop this character to create the CONFLICT OF GOALS.

We now have the "owners" of the goal and the counter goal. Now someone has to help the protagonist with reaching his goals, and someone has to interfere (in addition to the antagonist). This way we get protagonist's friends and enemies.

Stage 3. Protagonist's Friends and Enemies

The main thing you should know about friends: their efforts must be directed at helping the protagonist achieve his goal.

At the same time, to make the story exciting and eventful, someone has to be actively trying to prevent the hero from reaching his goal. This function is generally performed by the antihero, although there are usually some other "evil" characters as well. Thus we get protagonist's enemies and, mind you, they are not necessarily friends of the antagonist. They may not even know the antagonist, but whatever the reason may be, they will cause trouble for the protagonist and stand in his way.

When you have characters with the opposite goal vectors (some of them are directed towards the goal, others – against it) in the story, there will be ...

Stage 4. Actions and Reactions

And thus we have the complete structure of the story: its main events, conflicts, dialogues ... And it goes on and on until it's time for ...

Stage 5. The Final Battle

The last main battle between the protagonist and antagonist where only one of the opposing forces will be the winner, after which the story comes to its end.

These five stages clearly demonstrate that the story development and character development are inseparable and interdependent processes that complement each other.

Finally, the fourth and the last datum: **the main purpose of this technology is to develop your**

character so thoroughly that you could assume his POINT OF VIEW while writing the script. Then you will be able to make your character very ALIVE because his words and moves are going to be memorable, his actions will be LOGICAL, and more importantly, you will write the script in high gear.

We will come back to the principle of "assuming the character's point of view" at the end of this chapter, and now we will move on to the technology.

Below is the description of 13 steps for character development. You will need to do all of them for the protagonist. For the rest of the characters steps 6, 7, 10 and 13 are optional. Although you could use all 13 steps for any character in your story (it won't hurt).

The examples of each step in this chapter are given from the viewpoint of Julia (the protagonist's assistant from *The World of Insects*).

Note: *the technology described below should be used only after you thoroughly complete all the steps of the story development given in the first chapter.*

The Character Development Technology

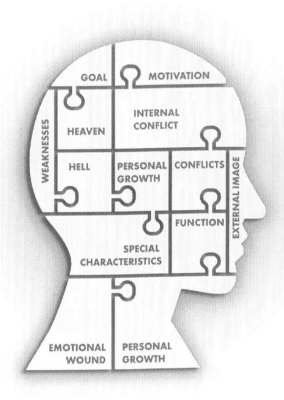

Step 1. Determine the character's Function

The starting point that all the subsequent steps will be based on is the character's FUNCTION.

Ask yourself the following questions:

1. Is the character's intention to HELP the protagonist reach his main goal or PREVENT him from that?

2. How is he going to pursue his intentions?

3. What is his role in the story?

EXAMPLE:

1. Julia's intention is to help Steve get out of "The World of Insects."

2. She will protect the main character in dangerous situations and help him overcome the obstacles.

3. Her influence will result in the change of the protagonist's character; she'll help him get out of "The World of Insects" and will contribute to his understanding of what the relationship between a man and a woman should be like, and the value of such a relationship.

Step 2. Set an exact GOAL for the character

After you've determined the character's role in your story in the previous step, you should define his **final objective** (it must be related to this story, not what he wants to achieve in life in general). Or you could determine the solution to his main problem.

When doing this step, remember that the GOAL is always something **specific** (like the key, the door, the exit, getting married, stealing the diamond, wiping the enemy off the face of the earth, etc.).

EXAMPLE: Julia's goal, which she will be working on throughout the story, is to obtain the antibodies to save her daughter's life and then get out of "The World of Insects" alive together with Steve.

Step 3. Describe the character's Motivation

Now find a clear motive that prompted your character to "get involved" in this story. Why, from the viewpoint of this character, must he perform his **function**?

Character's motivation is always internal. Motivation reveals his true nature and gives us a chance to see his inner world. Therefore, when developing a character, your primary task is to fully determine the MOTIVES of his ACTIONS.

Please note: motivation is not necessarily something that stays fixed throughout the story. Moreover, by changing the motivation you can clearly show the growth of your character as the story unfolds.

The key question to determine the character's motivation is: What makes him do what he does?

EXAMPLE: Julia is fighting for her daughter's life, so she is doing all she can to get the antibodies for the medicine. She also loves Steve and wants him to be happy, so she helps him every step of the way.

Step 4. Develop your character's "Heaven"

What are his dreams? What does he strive for? The character's "heaven" is often the same as what will happen when he reaches his goal, or when the main problem is solved.

Please note: the character's "HEAVEN" should be directly related to the events of the story, and not something generic like "becoming a millionaire" or "marrying a prince."

EXAMPLE: Saving her daughter's life, getting out of "The World of Insects," being with Steve for the rest of her life, publishing the results of their scientific research.

Step 5. Develop Your Character's "Hell"

What is his biggest fear? What is he trying to avoid at all costs? What will happen if he doesn't reach his goal or solve the main problem?

It is the situation, which he absolutely does not want to be in. Moreover, it's what could happen to him if he does not "get a move on" in the story.

EXAMPLE: Getting eaten by insects, letting her daughter die, Steve's death, Steve going back to his wife.

Step 6. Create the Emotional Wound

Here are some types of possible emotional wounds: "I want, but I can't," "I wanted, but I failed (did not work out)" or "things are not what I thought they were." Most often, it is a conflict of desire and opportunity. It could also be a major failure in the past that affects the current life and emotional state of the character.

EXAMPLE: Five years ago, when Steve was about to get married, Julia already knew that Mary would not make him happy. Julia also loved Steve and wanted to be with him, and she was sure that she could make him really happy. However, Julia was not brave and persistent enough to tell Steve at that time what she saw and felt and did not discourage that unhappy marriage. She has been blaming herself all these years for her lack of willpower and giving up, thus allowing those two people (and herself) to become unhappy.

Step 7. Devise The Internal Conflict

Internal conflict is a conflict of the person's desires (or intentions). This is what makes the character feel the tension, doubt and uncertainty about his further actions. **This is the problem of making the right choice.**

For example: keep going towards his goal or give up? Kill the enemy or let him live? Leave her husband or accept his infidelity? Keep supporting the good cause or cross over to the dark side?

Example: Julia dreams of being close to Steve, she wants to tell him about her feelings. However, starting a relationship with a married man is against her moral standards.

Step 8. Describe the Character's Strengths

The character's strong points are his traits, his abilities, knowledge, skills or areas of expertise that will **help** him reach his goals.

EXAMPLE: Julia does not panic in dangerous situations; she used to do mountain climbing; she continues to be analytical and move towards her goal even in the most challenging situations; she has a quick reaction and a lot of physical endurance.

Step 9. Describe the Character's Weaknesses

The character's weaknesses are those flaws that will slow him down while moving towards his objective.

EXAMPLE: Julia does not have enough courage to declare her feelings and opinions openly to the person she loves.

Step 10. Create the Character's Special Characteristics

Special characteristics are particular qualities of somebody or something. Character's special characteristics are usually developed in two stages. The first one is the creation of the internal characteristics; the second – external.

An internal characteristic is a trait, a hobby, a habit, etc., that influences the person's decisions and actions, and subsequently – the plot. An internal characteristic can be the same as one of the character's strong or weak points, or it can be a unique personality characteristic. It can frequently have a significant impact on the course of events and can lead to dramatic story twists.

EXAMPLE: Julia's internal characteristic is that she likes computer games. When lost in "The World of Insects," she feels the same "spirit of play" that she usually experiences while playing computer games. This allows her not to take everything too seriously and, in some ways, to even have fun and enjoy her adventures.

An external characteristic can be any detail of the character's appearance, of his facial expressions or motions. This is something that attracts attention to the character, makes him recognizable and different from the others. For example, a tattoo, haircut, particular look in his eyes, body type, sparkly ring, strange laughter, unusual facial expressions, etc.

EXAMPLE: Plump scarlet lips, no makeup, natural beauty.

Step 11. Create the Character's External Image

An image is a description that creates a vivid idea about someone. In our case, this is what the viewer will see on the screen: the appearance, style of clothing, age and other external features of the character.

EXAMPLE: Beautiful; short dark hair; athletic build; 28 years old.

Step 12. Work Out the Character's Conflicts

For the character to attract interest, it is necessary to introduce some other characters with whom he will be in conflict or have strong disagreements. A disagreement can manifest itself differently in different characters, but most often it leads to disputes, conflicts, upsets, quarrels or fights and can create a lot of either comic or tragic moments (depending on your genre). If your character is kind and not prone to conflict, well, figure out who and how will be suppressing him, who he will have to fight back if necessary, or who he will have to avoid throughout the story in order to not get into a great deal of trouble.

EXAMPLE: The main conflict, in which Julia is involved throughout the major part of the script, is the battle with giant insects. Besides, considering that Julia will be next to Steve all the time, we need to come up with some reason for them to have disagreements. That will allow us to make their dialogues exciting and imbue them with various emotions. Here are the reasons for disputes and conflicts between Julia and Steve: Steve doubts the reliability of the map that they found near the corpse. He thinks the map could be fake (i.e., it was given to that person with the purpose to entrap and destroy him) Nevertheless, Julia does all she can to make Steve move according to this map; she checks and verifies its reliability as they travel. Steve hesitates, Julia urges him on; he stops her from passing through dangerous (in his opinion) places, she "barges ahead" and sometimes even teases Steve for his indecisiveness. By the way, near the end of the story, this attitude towards Steve will get him to start facing the situations (instead of avoiding them) and reveal his masculine traits to the fullest.

Step 13. Work Out the Character's Personal Growth

In a screenplay, the protagonist, as well as some supporting characters, can (and ideally will) change. This usually happens when the character overcomes his weaknesses and acquires strengths. It may also be a change in the character's motivation or his philosophy and attitudes towards life. As a rule, the character's personal growth directly affects the development of the story (to get a better understanding of this – see the previous two chapters).

The key to the personal development is making the character grow and show "what he is made of" as a result of what happens to him in the story.

EXAMPLE: Julia's personal growth will be the transformation of her weakness into her strength. Her inability to tell Steve what she thinks about his relationship with Mary and his indecisiveness in life will turn into a strong ability to influence Steve and assist him in overcoming obstacles against all odds. Moreover, towards the end of the story, she will give him a piece of her mind concerning everything that has been accumulating inside of her over the years, which will finally get Steve to look at his life without any bias or excuses.

The character development can be considered complete at this point, although you can make certain additions to his characteristics throughout your entire work.

Now you have in your hands the technology that can bring your scriptwriting skills to an entirely new level.

Before you start using this technology, take the following rule as your guideline: **the INDICATOR that your character has been developed well is your ABILITY TO ASSUME HIS VIEWPOINT when writing the script.**

Having done all the steps of the character development, ask yourself the following questions:

• How does he think and act in various life situations?

• How does he achieve his goals?

• What does he talk to other people about and how?

You should be able to answer these and other similar questions without the slightest hesitation.

You must also be able to UNDERSTAND this character as well as you understand yourself. In other words, you must learn to BE him.

In this respect you will find it helpful to get in touch with a similar type of people or professionals, with the people who have similar problems to those of your character. Dive into that world, communicate, get familiar and collect the information relating to your character's life until you feel that you can really understand the people who are similar to your character.

You can also develop the ability to share the character's point of view through practice and exercises. It is easy and can actually be an interesting and unusual experience for you. To improve the skills of assuming the character's viewpoint I recommend you do the following: go for a walk and start looking at the environment, first through the eyes of one of your characters, then through the eyes of another, etc.

After spending some time in the role of each character, try quickly switching from one role to the other, from one character to the other, right then and there during your walk. After all, this is what you do while working on the script, isn't it? So why not master it?

I hope that I have presented everything in a clear and comprehensible way so that you can actually use this information. Although applying the principles described above may seem rather tricky to someone, when you know WHAT to do and HOW to do it, creating and bringing the characters to life is often a very enjoyable activity. And now you know it too.

The characters are waiting. Breathe LIFE into them. The story begins.

Checklist #3. The Character Development Technology

Step 1. Determine the character's FUNCTION

Step 2. Set an exact GOAL for the character

Step 3. Describe the character's MOTIVATION

Step 4. Develop your character's "HEAVEN"

Step 5. Develop your character's "HELL"

Step 6. Create the EMOTIONAL WOUND

Step 7. Devise the INTERNAL CONFLICT

Step 8. Describe the character's STRENGTHS

Step 9. Describe the character's WEAKNESSES

Step 10. Create the character's SPECIAL CHARACTERISTICS

Step 11. Create the character's EXTERNAL IMAGE

Step 12. Work out the character's CONFLICTS

Step 13. Work out the character's PERSONAL GROWTH

Chapter 4. How To Make The Story As Compelling As Possible

What is the difference between an ordinary, unremarkable story and the one that captivates the viewer in just a few minutes as if a powerful spell was cast over him? What makes a movie so enthralling that you cannot look away from the screen even for a couple of minutes until the resolution?

Imagine this: you start watching a movie that you've never heard of before and you don't know the actors in it. You haven't watched even half of it when something interrupts you, and you have to turn the TV off. What would this movie have to be like for you to keep wondering about it and want to finish watching it? Would it be just interesting? Or would the story have to resonate with you in such a way that even years later you would still be wondering about the ending?

I think you would agree with me that such stories exist, and I am not talking just about movies. It is for a good reason that some books become bestsellers, while others, even though the plot seems almost the same, remain known only to a small number of readers.

What we are dealing with here is a matter of interest or, to be more exact, the degree of interest. And this is what we are going to discuss in this chapter.

What is the **degree of interest**? In the dictionary we find the following definitions:

Degree — relative amount, level or extent of something.

Interest — specific attention to something, desire to understand the essence of the matter, to learn, to find out.

So in regard to the movies, we get the following definition: the degree of interest is the level of the viewer's involvement in the events that take place on the screen.

And this level can be either high — when you get this effect of not being able to look away, or low — when the audience can easily predict the next step of the protagonist and his opponent, and leaves the movie theatre on the thirty-fifth minute, bored. Therefore, we can draw a conclusion that any story will cause the viewer to have a certain degree of interest. That means that we, the scriptwriters, have *the opportunity to increase the viewer's interest.*

Our goal is to produce the stories that will be in the category of "the highest degree of the viewer's interest." To achieve this level, you need to be a true professional in developing exciting stories, as well as in using all those factors that lay the foundation for creating that kind of interest that keeps the viewer in his seat till the last seconds of the movie.

So let's proceed to the technology. There are six steps. If you do them thoroughly, they will maximize the "degree of the viewer's interest."

Once again, the examples for each step will be based on *The World of Insects* story.

Step 1. Ask the "Main Question"

It's human nature that any secret or suspense captures one's attention in some mystical way. A mystery is something that a person just can't make peace with, so one's attention will always focus on questions and uncertainties.

93

When we talk about using "questions" in a movie, this is the cornerstone of creating and controlling interest. Moreover, if the "principle of questions" is used correctly, you will provide the greatest enjoyment and satisfaction for your viewers.

As an example, think of the secrets of the ancient civilizations. What historical events cause the most controversy? Usually those that have some unknown details, where something is missed, hidden or lost. Therefore people have the opportunity to imagine how "it could have been" and fill in the gaps with some information. A good example of this is the Egyptian pyramids. Centuries have passed, but the excitement around this great mystery has not abated. There is one, and only one, reason for that – the human mind needs ANSWERS. The "mental computer" tries to automatically solve any riddle that you give to it. If we take this principle of the human mind as a basis, we get a fantastic opportunity to create exciting stories.

So here is the first step: INTRODUCE THE "MAIN QUESTION" INTO THE STORY.

This is the question that the viewer will try to answer throughout the whole movie.

Here are some simple examples of such questions: Will they stay together or break up after all? Will the protagonist manage to deactivate the bomb or not? Will the protagonist escape from prison, and if yes, how? Will the heroes save their planet from invaders? Will she avenge her parents' death?

Important note: the question is created, first of all, for the viewer. Of course, at the same time, this question can be for the protagonist as well. For example, in *The Matrix* Neo tries to understand whether he is the chosen one and the viewer looks for the answer together with him.

There is also another option, where the protagonist has no mystery while the viewer does. At the beginning of the movie we see the "scene of protagonist's death" and then we see the words "One year earlier" and then we watch the whole movie asking ourselves, "How on earth has the hero got himself into that awful last scene if everything is going so well right now?" (We are going to return to this example at the end of this chapter)

As the next example let's take the *Titanic*. A love story is born aboard the ship. BUT we know that an inevitable disaster is coming, and the viewer asks the "main question": will the heroes survive the disaster; will they stay together? He will be trying to answer this question throughout the whole movie.

"How is it going to end?" "Who will be the winner?" "Who will get the first prize?" These are the kinds of questions that a screenwriter has to be able to pose in his screenplay at the very beginning of his work. If you are currently writing a screenplay, just ask yourself, "What is the 'main question' that the viewer will be trying to answer throughout the movie?" Your answer, believe me, is worth its weight in gold. Based on the answer create a "game" of solving a mystery for the viewer for those 1.5-2 hours that he will spend in front of the screen.

While creating the "main question" you should also keep in mind the following rule: the sooner you put the main mystery in place, the faster the viewer will get involved in your story. Therefore, do not hesitate to introduce the main mystery in the first few minutes of the movie. Never delay using this screenplay technique. If you haven't used it before the first plot point – it is too late. By then you should be able to introduce at least 2-3 more mysteries into your story.

You can come up with a great number of various "questions." There are as many kinds of mysteries that could be created as there are stories and their authors. Nevertheless, one thing is for sure: mystery is what makes the viewers "glued" to the screens, and the readers — to the books. Analyze the movies that you consider the most fascinating and see for yourself.

Step 2. Create The "Mystery Hooks"

By "mystery hooks" we mean various secrets that your story needs to be packed with. It is an excellent auxiliary tool for the scriptwriter to maintain constant interest of the viewers. It is the "hooks" that make the viewer ask himself such questions as "What's happening?", "Who has really done it, after all?" or "Did he go down the wrong path again?"... The "mystery hooks" strategically placed throughout the story keep reminding the viewer that there is still much to be revealed and many questions have not been answered yet.

For example, we can use the "hooks" to indicate that one of the characters secretly communicates with someone and nobody on his team knows about it (or, on the contrary, somebody does know about it but cannot ask directly). Who does he communicate with? Is he a traitor or is he trying to get more help? This mystery can be solved by either the viewer or one of the main characters.

Important: the "mystery hooks" introduced into the screenplay will not only captivate the viewer but will also make the viewer's mind stay alert throughout the story. Have you watched (or read) The Da Vinci Code or Harry Potter?

Do you see what I mean? The viewer truly enjoys the story when we completely immerse him in the events. To achieve this effect, it is essential to provide him with the opportunity to think together with the protagonist, analyze, make guesses, solve mysteries.

And now let's get to the point, or to be more exact, to the technology. If you simply start telling the story in the tiniest of details, the viewer could get bored within the first five minutes. That's why we take a different approach — we begin the narration by hiding the key elements. However ... we also drop some hints.

Hints indirectly indicate certain facts or circumstances but do not give us the full understanding of the situation. It piques the viewer's interest to find the solution or the answer to such questions as "What is it?" or "Where will it lead?" Therefore such hints act as the main "mystery hooks" for the audience.

Here are some simple examples of the "hooks": a shadow slipping around the corner of the house, a fortune teller's prediction, a strange dream, a sudden disappearance of the main character's assistant, etc.

Summary: after you've worked on the first stages of the story development described in the previous chapters, you need to fill it with the "hooks" in order to capture the viewer's interest and then masterfully maintain it up to the resolution of the story.

EXAMPLE:

The "mystery hooks" used in the story about Steve are as follows:

1. Rumor has it that people go missing in "The World of Insects"... Is that true?

2. Steve and Julia's radios and tracking devices stop working ... Is it a coincidence or is there someone behind that?

3. What is a scavenger insect doing there?

Step 3. Create The "Keys"

A "key" is the information that was obtained, the mystery that was solved or a certain object that the character needs as a "pass" for the next stage of the story.

In other words, the "keys" are something that allows the characters to achieve intermediate goals on their way to the desired outcome. In this step (when you are creating the "keys"), you need to fully work out what information your character will need to receive on his way to the goal, the main mysteries he will have to solve, the objects he'll need to get or the persons he'll have to ally with in order to achieve his objectives.

For example, he will need to: figure out the code to the safety deposit box; find the enemy's location; trick the antagonist's mistress into telling him the enemy's secrets, etc.

You could say that by obtaining each subsequent "key" the hero is now able to overcome the next obstacle that was stopping him before on his way to the goal.

As the characters move along the story, they must solve even bigger mysteries, obtain the information that is more valuable, gain the objects that are more meaningful to their victory. They must collect the "keys" that become more and more important to them as their quest progresses.

In the next step you will find out the connection between the "keys" and maintaining the viewer's interest.

EXAMPLE:

1. Steve and Julia find a hunting map and a navigation device, which makes it possible for them to locate themselves in "The World of Insects" and determine the direction of the exit.

2. Characters discover and capture a valuable insect (they think it may be the carrier of the antibodies for the deadly virus).

3. Tests show that this insect is indeed the carrier of the antibodies, and now the characters not only have to save themselves, they must also bring this insect with them, whatever it takes (capturing the insect and the positive test results take the story to the next level).

Step 4. Create Complicated Ways Of Obtaining The "Keys"

We will start with a bit of theory on the purpose of the "keys" and how obtaining them is related to strengthening the viewer's interest.

Here's the secret. When you know exactly WHAT all the "keys" to the new levels of your story are, you can make the process of getting each key into a separate "mini-adventure." And here is another important principle: *the characters must work hard to obtain the "keys." It should not be simply "I came, I saw, I conquered." It must be difficult for them.*

Your viewer should feel again and again throughout the film, that the protagonist is at the breaking point, that he is about to lose, that "this time he will definitely fail."

If you make sure that the characters are looking death in the eye every time they obtain another "key," the viewer (who is going to be on the edge of his seat throughout the movie) would want to embrace you at the end.

There is a perfect example of that in the *Mission Impossible* movie when Tom Cruise's character is hanging down from the ceiling. Anyone who has seen it at least once will never forget it.

The rule of this step is: create the circumstances with the highest risk for your character because the VIEWER'S INVOLVEMENT in the story is directly proportionate to the CHARACTER'S RISK in each scene.

You need to also learn to create the SUSPENSE. Use the following screenplay techniques for that:

1. The danger is getting close while the character is not aware of it. In this case, the viewer sees a real danger

threatening the hero (but the hero himself does not see it at that moment), and asks the question, "Is it possible that this time he will be able to get out of it unscathed? Or is he a dead man now?" This is one of the most powerful techniques for getting the viewer involved in the story. For example, the protagonist sneaks into the enemy's house to obtain some secret information. While he tries to copy the data onto his USB drive, we see his enemy drive up to the house unexpectedly and now quickly approaching the front door. "The hero is in danger! What will happen now?!" the viewer exclaims in his mind swallowing the "screenplay bait" in a split second.

2. The inability of the protagonist or his supporters to make a decision in a dangerous situation. In this case, the viewer is aware of the danger for the character, but the resolution of the situation is delayed because of the character's suspicion or fear of something. Thus the antagonist (or another threat) gets closer every second, and the situation becomes more and more dangerous, but the hesitating protagonist takes his time, thereby increasing the viewers' interest and emotional tension. For example, at a critical moment of the story the protagonist is standing on the river bank, hesitating to jump in and cross over to the other side (although this is his only way out) because he knows that there are crocodiles in the river. Meanwhile, the antagonist is closing in on him from behind. Just a few more minutes – and it will be too late for the hero to jump into the water because he will be dead. "Jump, swim!" the viewer whispers and the emotional tension gets higher and higher every second.

3. The danger is getting closer, but the protagonist has no data for making his decision. This is very similar to the situation described in the previous paragraph, except in this case the protagonist cannot jump into action because he lacks the necessary information. There is no data on what to do now or which way to go. For example, our hero is lost in a dangerous labyrinth. At that moment the antagonist sees him and starts moving toward him with a gun in his hand. However the protagonist is not in a hurry to run away from the threat – instead he is looking at the map, trying to determine where the exit is. At this point, the viewer feels the tension and shouts to himself (and sometimes out loud), "Come on! Quick! The evil is near! Run!"

And one more important thing: when you make the protagonist work hard and struggle for each "key," you get the viewer involved in the story through his empathy with the hero. By the way, to get the highest level of empathy you need to alternate the character's failures with his victories that he will have thanks to his persistence, strength, intelligence and abilities.

Recall the *Indiana Jones* movies or the *Gladiator* — we empathize with the protagonists of these stories because of the injustice and failures they face, then we admire their courage, strength and intelligence, and after that we empathize with them again ... And this goes on throughout the whole movie. It works perfectly, making the viewer "join the game" and fight on the side of the main character.

Analyze any great protagonist in a well-known story and look for this factor – you will be surprised that there is always some empathy with the protagonist because of the injustice and failures in his difficult path. We also feel admiration for his actions and deeds.

EXAMPLE:

1. In the tunnel Steve and Julia find a hunting map and a navigation device near the skeleton. At that moment they see a spider and now they not only have to get out of the tunnel and keep their findings safe, they also must get rid of the spider before it kills them. Julia gets trapped in a web and Steve rescues her after shooting the spider. For the first time, he is able to overcome his weakness (the inability to kill an insect) in this scene, which is really hard for him.

2. After that they see an insect that Steve thinks could be the carrier of the antibodies for the virus. With great difficulty our heroes manage to catch it.

3. Now, they need to find out whether this insect really carries the antibodies. Steve is going to do the test, but at that moment they get attacked by another poisonous spider who tries to snatch the valuable insect from them. The heroes manage to escape with the insect, but Julia injures her leg in the battle, and it is now more difficult for her to move around.

Step 5. Devise the "Increasing Pressure Of The Circumstances"

Your task is to inexorably increase the opposition to the protagonist and his goals every minute. The problems must become more and more complicated, and the main threat must be getting closer and closer.

To get a better understanding of how to do this step masterfully, imagine that your protagonist is running towards his GOAL down a long road. ALL the events of your story are happening to him along this road, from the exposition to the resolution. In other words, the road represents the complete path that your hero has to travel.

Now imagine that this road is held in a vise. And from the very first minutes of the movie it is slowly but continuously getting tighter and tighter. This vise would be that "ever-increasing pressure of the circumstances."

I'm going to list here just a few ways that can help you create such "pressure" in your script:

1. **Increase the number of people who "play against" the protagonist**.

2. **Loss of tools, weapons or abilities necessary for achieving his goal** (or simply for protection) – take away any opportunity, ability or a valuable tool from the protagonist.

3. **Add something that impedes the protagonist.** For example, an injury to one of his supporters who now needs to be carried and the lack of possibility to leave him in a safe place.

4. **Conflict with his supporters** (loss or departure of one or more of them).

5. **Increase the number of obstacles** (a lot of various barriers).

6. **Increase the difficulty of obstacles** (few obstacles, however, they are almost insurmountable).

As the protagonist travels further "down the road," the risk of his complete defeat must be increasing and the chances of winning decreasing. Each following action of the protagonist should require more and more courage because of the growing opposition of the "forces of evil."

As the story unfolds, it is also important to make it harder and harder for the protagonist to turn back or retreat. Also try creating the pressure of time by limiting the possibility of achieving the goal within the time frame. For example, the antagonist is going to show up in 10 minutes, so the protagonist must get the safe open before that. Some more examples: the plane leaves in an hour; at midnight the carriage turns into a pumpkin; there are only three days to pay the debt, etc.

You will notice that by increasing the pressure of circumstances consistently, you widen the gap between what the hero must do, and what he can do.

Therefore, when you create the adventure for your main character, destroy his possibilities and create "impossibilities." In this case he must give it his all, physically and mentally. He uses all his energy and ... this energy becomes contagious for the viewer! After all, you've probably noticed that the more effort and work you put in your goal, the sweeter and longer-lasting is the taste of the victory.

The same goes for the movie. Every victory of the protagonist is the viewer's victory. The more obstacles the hero overcomes on his way to the goal, the more energy he uses, the more we empathize with him and eventually, the more we rejoice over his final victory. That is why a truly well-made movie is inspiring.

EXAMPLE:
1. Insects are attacking the characters from all directions.
2. The need to safeguard the valuable insect — the source of antibodies.
3. The search party leader is sent to "The World of Insects" on a mission to kill Steve and Julia.
4. Julia's daughter is very sick, and they need to get back in time to save her.

5. Characters are running out of the antidote, food and water.
6. Steve and Julia cannot sleep at the same time. They need to alternate so that one of them is always alert.
7. The antagonist releases insects that are extremely dangerous.

Step 6. Introduce Surprises and Unexpected Twists Into the Story

After you have immersed the viewer in the story and succeeded in getting him (with the techniques described above) to continually analyze and guess what happens next, you then need to make the viewer disappointed every time he tries to predict the events because he guessed wrong! If you are going to meet the viewer's expectations – he will simply lose interest in your story, but if you surprise him – he will worship you.

The use of unexpected twists in a screenplay always produces an effect. It shakes the viewer up a bit and makes him experience emotions. However, you decide what emotions the viewer is going to feel at that moment — be it frustration, anger or joy.

If you do this step correctly, you will not let the viewer get used to the story and let him think about anything else. When creating those surprises and twists, your objective is to make the viewer happy, surprised or scared so that you would hear things like, "Holy mackerel! Who would have thought that ... ," etc.

A surprise could be a revealed secret, unexpected outside assistance, meeting with a sweetheart, or betrayal of a friend at the worst possible time. It can either be pleasant or on the contrary – really aggravate the protagonist's situation.

To do this step masterfully, you need to learn one of the key screenplay techniques: the hero will be taking a lot of various actions throughout the story and expect certain results. You need to make sure that each time the result is not exactly what he expected, and not what the viewer predicted. It does not mean that the hero should lose where he needs to win, but it does mean that the victory should not be as quick and easy as he thought it would be.

Even when you give the viewer the answer to "the main question," ideally it should be something quite opposite to what he was expecting. And the greater the difference is between what he expected and what he eventually finds out, the stronger the effect will be.

Do you remember the example I gave you earlier, where at the beginning of the movie we see the scene of the "protagonist's death" and then we see the words "One year earlier"? And we watch the movie asking ourselves, "How on earth has the hero got himself into that awful last scene if everything is going so well right now?"

I promised to come back to this example at the end of the chapter. Using the screenplay commandment "Thou shalt not let thy viewer's predictions come true," we make the following move: towards the end of the story when it's time for the scene of the "protagonist's death," we start showing this scene, cut it short, and then we show that this scene was in the protagonist's mind. Those were his thoughts when he was contemplating what could happen to his life if he didn't get his act together.

Having realized that the risk is too high, our hero takes control of his life, goes all-out and creates a different outcome, completely opposite to the one that the viewer expected to see.
EXAMPLE:

1. Michael turns out to be the CEO of "The World of Insects."

2. Sudden failure of the tracking devices and walkie-talkies.

3. First time when the characters fall into the tunnel.

4. A human skeleton with a bullet hole in its skull.

5. More skeletons in another tunnel.

6. The leader of the search party gets unexpectedly killed by his former assistant.

7. A dangerous insect suddenly devours Michael.

These are simple but at the same time, rather tricky techniques to "immerse" your viewer into the story.

The "mystery hooks," the "keys," the increasing pressure of circumstances, the surprises and twists are all invaluable tools you can use when writing a story.

Use them, practice, perfect your skills and create truly EXCITING STORIES.

Checklist #4. Making the StoryCompelling

STEP 1. ASK THE "MAIN QUESTION"

This is the question that the viewer will try to answer throughout the whole movie.

STEP 2. CREATE THE "MYSTERY HOOKS"

By "mystery hooks" we mean various secrets that your story needs to be packed with.

STEP 3. CREATE THE "KEYS"

A "key" is the information that was obtained, the mystery that was solved or a certain object that the character needs as a "pass" for the next stage of the story.

STEP 4. CREATE COMPLICATED WAYS OF OBTAINING THE "KEYS"

Here's the secret. When you know exactly WHAT all the "keys" to the new levels of your story are, you can make the process of getting each key into a separate "mini-adventure." And here is another important principle: *the characters must work hard to obtain the "keys." It should not be simply "I came, I saw, I conquered." It must be difficult for them.*

STEP 5. DEVISE THE "INCREASING PRESSURE OF THE CIRCUMSTANCES"

Here are some ways that can help you create such "pressure" in your script:

- **Increase the number of people who "play against" the protagonist**.

- **Loss of tools, weapons or abilities necessary for achieving his goal** (or simply for protection) – take away any opportunity, ability or a valuable tool from the protagonist.
- **Add something that impedes the protagonist.** For example, an injury to one of his supporters who now needs to be carried and the lack of possibility to leave him in a safe place.
- **Conflict with his supporters** (loss or departure of one or more of them).
- **Increase the number of obstacles** (a lot of various barriers).
- **Increase the difficulty of obstacles** (few obstacles, however, they are almost insurmountable).

STEP 6. Introduce Surprises and Unexpected Twists Into the Story

Chapter 5. The Story-Flash Game

The greatest danger for an artist is being too serious!

That seriousness always comes from the thought "I can fail, I am not going to succeed..."

Of course, anyone (especially someone who creates new universes with their imagination) could have experienced in the past a lot of criticism and invalidation from others, failures, and stops.

Our environment often imposes a certain course of action upon us. We frequently hear: "Do this, think like that..." or "See how successful other people are – and you are not..." and so on. This results in a serious attitude towards life; the creative simplicity and ease inherent in artists go away.

Start using the Story-Flash Game and eliminate the seriousness and strain from your creativity!

Perhaps, you have been creating something for so long that at some point you stop enjoying it.

The Story-Flash Game will bring your joy of creation back!

It will help you remove the "stops" and creativity-related doubts from your mind. In a short time, you will be able to clear up your imagination from the barriers!

Here is the law that will help you eliminate the complexity and create more:

If things are stuck, start creating something noncommittal, with no strings attached.

That is why the Story-Flash game was created.

Just start creating and "wasting" ideas! Lots of ideas!

This is a "What If?" type of a game.

For example, what if we combine in the same story: a millionaire, a secretary, and a plane ticket? What if we give the secretary mind-reading powers and make the millionaire blind? And then introduce the "need to escape" to the mix?

You will be surprised how quickly the story starts moving forward with just a few initial components!

To make the game easy and fun I developed a hundred cards.

All you need to do is to take a hundred pieces of paper and simply write their titles (as given below), or you could even draw them if you want.

You will have five sets of cards with different categories (20 cards in each):

- **Characters**

- **Objects**

- **Skills/Abilities**

- **Flaws/Disabilities**

- **Plot twists**

CHARACTERS

1. Policeman
2. Musician
3. Writer
4. Artist
5. Secretary
6. Millionaire
7. Cab driver
8. Racing driver
9. Traveler
10. Pilot
11. Student
12. Teacher
13. Programmer
14. Actress
15. Boxer
16. Cleaning lady
17. Singer
18. Businessman
19. Nurse
20. Hacker

OBJECTS

1. Phone
2. Swiss army knife
3. Backpack with lots of various things
4. Clock
5. Car
6. Handgun
7. Invisibility cloak
8. Map
9. Laptop
10. Key to all doors
11. Ballpoint pen
12. Rope
13. Sleeping pills
14. Bicycle
15. Binoculars
16. Matches
17. Rollerblades
18. Chewing gum
19. Gold bar
20. Plane ticket

SKILLS/ABILITIES

1. Great dancer
2. Can makes others fall in love with him/her easily
3. Cooks well
4. Good painter
5. Sings beautifully
6. Knows martial arts
7. Good driver
8. Skilled programmer
9. Fast runner
10. Can make money easily
11. Can impersonate anybody
12. Super memory
13. Knows a lot of languages
14. Risk-taker
15. Mind-reading powers
16. Great physical strength
17. Can see through walls
18. Attentive and observant
19. Healing powers
20. Can hack others' computers

FLAWS/DISABILITIES

1. Blind

2. Deaf

3. Can't read

4. Afraid of computers

5. Doesn't like to take showers

6. Eats too much

7. Afraid of darkness

8. Lazy

9. Quickly spends all their money

10. Can't keep secrets

11. Has no friends

12. Afraid of animals

13. Too amorous

14. Afraid to make decisions

15. Doesn't trust anyone

16. Too trusting

17. Absentminded

18. Illiterate

19. Afraid of public speaking

20. Too talkative

PLOT TWISTS

1. Danger

2. Love

3. Surprise

4. Disease

5. Theft

6. Business trip

7. Escape

8. New goal

9. Betrayal

10. Deception

11. Adultery

12. Inheritance

13. Pregnancy

14. Injury

15. Big winnings

16. Strange neighbor

17. Prediction

18. New business partner

19. False accusation

20. Lookalike

You can play this game by yourself or with others.
You can simply create stories or have a challenge: who comes up with a brilliant plot first.

To begin with, you should make a hundred cards and divide them into five categories. One pile will have the "Characters," another "Disabilities/Flaws," next one "Skills/Abilities" and so on.

Then draw the first six cards: the protagonist and antagonist from the "Characters" stack, and from the other stacks – the object, the ability, the disability and the plot twist.

After that, you simply follow the Checklist #1 "STEPS OF CREATING THE STORY" and create your story.

To make it more interesting you can take additional characters or objects cards, but on the condition that you must use the object that you drew. The same with the characters – the one you get must play a role in the story. He/she has to help either the protagonist or antagonist or play some other secondary part in the story.

You can also draw additional abilities or disabilities for your protagonist and/or antagonist. Just have fun with the cards and use your imagination to the fullest.

After a while, you will realize that you can create stories very easily and that you can work miracles with the initial set of story components you didn't think you possibly could!

Checklists will help you do that.

When you have developed your story according to Checklist #1 and have the basic outline, you can start structuring the story with the help of Checklist #2.

Then you develop your characters with Checklist #3.

Later you could add tension to your story by using Checklist #4.

Here's an example of playing the Game.

You draw six cards:

Two from the "characters" pile and one from each of the other four piles.

Let's say you get the following cards:

Your main character is a millionaire.

The antagonist is a secretary.

The disability is blindness.

The ability is mind-reading powers.

The object is a plane ticket.

The plot twist is escape.

Now just start creating a story based on these six cards and the steps of Checklist #1.

Let's take Checklist #1 and start.

STEP 1. In a few sentences, describe the PRIMARY SITUATION, in which the protagonist has found himself and which he must successfully handle.

Working with the cards we drew (all six can be used but that is not necessary), we get the following **primary situation**:

A blind millionaire is about to lose his fortune when he goes on a trip with his secretary, unaware that she can read his mind and wants to embezzle all his money. Soon his infatuation turns into fear, and now he needs to escape from this nightmare vacation.

STEP 2. Create the PROTAGONIST. Here is what you need to know at this stage of your work: the character must be created based on his goals and intentions.

The goal (it's always something specific) is to keep his money safe from the cunning secretary.

The intention (desire, aspiration) is to stay affluent and successful.

STEP 3. Describe the knowledge, skills and abilities of your protagonist (everything related to his ability to confront the challenges and solve problems).

Since we decided to use the card with the mind-reading ability to empower the antagonist, we need to come up with another ability for the millionaire, or you could take a new card from the "abilities" pile. Don't forget that each card you draw must be used.

Let's say we can't think of an ability, so we take a new card – having "super memory."

STEP 4. Give the protagonist some tools that will help him achieve his goals (it can be a device, gadget or weapon).

Here we use the "plane ticket" (as we previously drew this card from the "objects" pile) or we could come up with something else that will help our hero achieve his goal.

STEP 5. Devise the emotional wound for the protagonist.

Let's use our imagination here: he loves traveling but after he went blind, he can enjoy his trips nowhere near as much as before, which makes him very unhappy.

STEP 6. Give the protagonist a flaw. This is something that could mess up his plans, something that could jeopardize his victory.

We have the "disability/flaw" – blindness; but you could come up with another one, for example, "trusts his secretary too much," or you could take an additional disability/flaw card from the stack.

STEP 7. Now, create **the main ANTAGONIST**. It's a person (or creature) who will oppose the protagonist. Create him based on his goals and intentions.

The secretary. Her goal is to take all her boss's money. Her intention is to be rich and never have to work again.

And so on.

Have fun with the checklists, by yourself or with your friends!

By the way, I recommend you use the Story-Flash Workbooks for the game and make your notes right there. It is very convenient, but most importantly – you will keep all the brilliant ideas you came up with! More information in chapter About The Story-Flash Workbook.

Through playing this game you will be able to master the Story-Flash technology, but most importantly – you will stop taking the process of creating stories too seriously. As a result, you are going to be able to come up with stories quickly, easily and have fun!

The game will help you understand the "mechanics" of creating stories and see the most important principles of building the plot. You will also have fun! And above all – the barriers to your imagination will be smashed to smithereens, and you will feel inspired to write again!

Play and create!

Chapter 6. Story-Flash Exercises

Exercises for Chapter 1

Before starting these exercises, pick one of your favorite movies and watch it again.

Do the following exercises:

Exercise: Primary Situation
Describe the primary situation of this film.
Try to do it in five sentences.

Exercise: Creating the Protagonist
Describe the protagonist's goal.
What does he want to achieve?
Describe his intentions (what he wants to do and what he is trying to avoid).

Exercise: Protagonist's Skills
List the knowledge, skills and abilities of the protagonist.

Exercise: Protagonist's Tools
List the tools of the protagonist in the movie.

Exercise: Emotional Wound
Determine the "emotional wound" of the protagonist.
Describe how it affects his personality and actions.

Exercise: Protagonist's Flaw

Find and name the protagonist's flaw.

Describe how this flaw can prevent him from achieving his goals.

Exercise: Creating the Antagonist

Who is the antagonist in this film?

Describe his goal precisely. What does he want to achieve?

Describe the antagonist's intentions (what he wants to do and what he is he trying to avoid).

Exercise: Antagonist's Abilities

Describe what makes the antagonist invincible, unpredictable and talented.

Exercise: Reason for Confrontation

What is the main conflict between the protagonist and the antagonist?

Determine the reason for the protagonist's opposition to the antagonist.

Why does one resist the other so furiously?

Exercise: A Spoke in the Wheel

List how the antagonist puts a spoke in the protagonist's wheel. What barriers does he create?

Exercise: Goals of the Secondary Characters

Make a list of several friends of the protagonist in the movie.

Describe their intentions and goals.

List the several enemies of the protagonist. Describe their intentions and goals.

Exercise: Plot Outline
Recall and describe the plot of the movie dividing it into three parts – the beginning, the middle part and the ending.

Exercise: Secondary Conflicts
Describe the secondary conflicts of this film.

Exercise: Antipathy towards the Antagonist
Describe the negative actions done by the antagonist. Specify why these actions cause feelings of dislike towards him.

Exercise: Punishment for the Antagonist
Describe the antagonist's punishments.
What exactly makes the viewer rejoice?
What is the triumph of justice in this case?

Exercise: Reward for the Protagonist
Describe what the protagonist receives for his hard work.
Specify why it is valuable and important to him.

Exercise: Threat
Describe the threats that are hanging over the hero.
Specify the greatest danger.
Describe how the threat continues hanging over the hero throughout the story, forcing him to be more proactive in order to achieve his purpose.

Exercise: Protagonist's Change

Describe how exactly the protagonist changes in the movie. Determine why the change in the protagonist brings out emotions in the viewers.

Exercise: Secondary Line

Describe the secondary plot lines of this film. Determine how they create additional depth for the story.

Exercise: Protagonist's Development

Describe who (or what) helps the hero acquire new knowledge and experience.

Why is this knowledge important to him? What difference does it make for the events of the story?

Exercise: Legend

If the film you chose includes a legend, describe it in several sentences. Indicate how it immerses the viewer into the story.

Exercises for Chapter 2

Note: *I recommend that for these exercises you choose a film the structure of which you would like to study in detail.*

Exercise: Exposition

1. *Watch the beginning of the movie you have chosen.*
2. *Describe the exposition in several sentences.*
3. *Name the actions used by the screenwriter to introduce the protagonist to us.*

Exercise: Inciting Incident

    4. Find the "inciting incident" in the film you have chosen.

    5. Describe how this incident sends the protagonist on a journey. How exactly does he get pulled into the "game"?

Exercise: Orientation Period

    1. Determine when the orientation period begins and ends in the movie.

    2. What does the protagonist learn during this period?

Exercise: First Plot Point

    1. Find the "first plot point" in the film you have chosen.

    2. Describe why this event is a powerful impetus for the entire second act.

Exercise: Adjustment Period

    Determine when the adjustment period begins and ends in the movie.

    What does the protagonist do during this period? How does he adjust to the circumstances?

Exercise: Main Turning Point

    1. Find the "main turning point" in the film you have chosen.

    2. Describe why this is the point where the hero becomes more of a master of the situation rather than a person who is "going with the flow."

    3. Describe how the protagonist "burns all his bridges" (if that does take place in the movie)

Exercise: Action Period

1. *Determine when the action period begins and when it ends.*

2. *What does the protagonist do during this period? Describe all his actions.*

3. *Specify HOW the principle of "every action has an equal and opposite reaction" is used to create the confrontation between the protagonist and antagonist. What does the antagonist do to react to the protagonist's actions?*

Exercise: Second Plot Point

1. *Determine the "second plot point" in the film you have chosen.*

2. *Describe why this event is a "big failure."*

3. *Determine what makes this event a catalyst for the conflict and tension.*

Exercise: Protagonist's Crisis

1. *Determine the protagonist's crisis in the film you have chosen.*

2. *Describe the choice that the hero has to make.*

3. *What makes this moment a test of the hero's willpower and integrity?*

4. *How exactly does the protagonist's modus operandi change because of this crisis?*

Exercise: Final Battle

1. *Describe the final battle in the film you have chosen.*

2. What ideals clash in this battle (lies vs. truth, being dependent on a rich husband vs. freedom, friendship vs. betrayal, etc.)?

Exercise: Climax

1. Determine the climax of the film you have chosen.
2. Describe the victory of the principles that the protagonist was fighting for (if it is not a drama and the hero is victorious).

Exercise: Resolution

In this exercise you need to work thoroughly on all four points described in this step:

1. Find the moment that demonstrates the value of the victory for the protagonist. Describe how he enjoys the win (if it is shown).
2. How can we see that the victory is final, and the evil is not likely to come back?
3. Describe the moment (the scene) that shows the change in the protagonist's life after his victory over evil.
4. How does this movie show (if it does) that the hero's ideals are now a reality?

Exercise: Timeline

Create the TIMELINE for the film you have chosen.
Yes, it is not going to be too easy or quick, but this exercise will allow you to see the entire structure of the film. Such an exercise will help you gain a "professional's point of view." It is like practice for a surgeon — nobody will let

him touch a patient until he demonstrates his competence in a controlled environment.

Would you like to learn how to "see" the structure of successful films? Then do this exercise!

Exercise: Episode Plan

Create the episode plan for the film you have chosen.

Exercise: Elements that Advance the Plot

Find the elements that advance the plot in each episode of your episode plan.

Exercise: List of Episodes

Make a list of all episodes in the film you have chosen and give them names.

Exercises for Chapter 3

Exercise: Character's Function

Choose three characters from the movie you have just watched. Describe each of them as follows:

1. What are his intentions? Does he interfere with the protagonist achieving his goal or does he help him?
2. What methods does he use to pursue his intentions?
c. What is his role in the story? Why was he introduced into the story?

Exercise: Character's Goal

Describe the GOALS of the three characters you have chosen.

Exercise: Motivation

1. Describe the MOTIVATION of the three characters you have chosen.
2. WHY must each of them perform his **function**? WHAT is his reason for that?
3. Determine whether the motivation of those characters changes as the story unfolds.

Exercise: Character's "Heaven"

Describe the "HEAVEN" of the characters you have chosen the way you see it. Answer these questions about each character: What does he dream about? What does he strive for?

Exercise: Character's "Hell"

Describe the "HELL" of the characters you have chosen the way you see it. Answer these questions about each character: What is his biggest fear? What is he trying to avoid at all costs? What will happen if he doesn't reach his goal or solve the main problem?

Exercise: Character's Emotional Wound

1. Describe the emotional wounds of the characters you have chosen.

2. Determine "the conflict of desire and opportunities," if any.

Exercise: Internal Conflict

Usually only the protagonist has an internal conflict. Therefore, return to the protagonist you chose for the Chapter 1 exercises and determine his internal conflict.

Exercise: Character's Strengths

Let's go back to the three characters you have chosen for the exercises of this chapter.

1. Describe their strong points.
2. Determine which of these strong points help each character achieve their goals.

Exercise: Character's Weaknesses

1. Describe the weak points of each character you have chosen.
2. Determine how these weak points impede each character in achieving his goals.

Exercise: Internal Characteristics

1. Identify and describe the internal characteristics of each character you have chosen.
2. Do the internal characteristics influence the story?
3. Identify and describe the external characteristics of each character.

Exercise: External Image

Describe in detail the appearance of the characters you have chosen.

Note: If necessary, do this exercise in front of the screen while looking at the character you are describing.

Exercise: Conflicts

1. Describe the conflicts that involve the characters you have chosen.
2. Specify the reason for each conflict.

Exercise: Character's Personal Growth

1. Determine if the characters you have chosen experience personal growth.

2. If yes, describe it.

3. Describe the reasons for the personal growth also.

Exercises for Chapter 4

Exercise: The Main Question
Identify and write down the "main question" of the movie you have chosen.

Exercise: The Hooks
1. *Find and describe the "hooks" in the movie you have chosen.*
2. *Write down the question the viewer is asking himself as a result of each "hook."*

Exercise: The Keys
1. *Find the "keys" in the movie you have chosen.*
2. *Describe why the protagonist would not be able to move further without at least one of the keys, in other words, why the plot would get stuck in that case.*

Exercise: Obtaining the Keys
1. *In the movie you have chosen, determine which "keys" the protagonist gets easily and which he obtains with great difficulty.*
2. *Describe the dangers the protagonist had to face in those scenes where the key was hard to get.*
3. *Think of some other ways that would make obtaining the "keys" even more complicated.*

Exercise: Pressure of Circumstances

Describe how the "increasing pressure of the circumstances" is represented in the movie you have chosen.

Note: *When doing this exercise, keep in mind the six ways of creating the "pressure" listed in Chapter 4 but do not limit yourself to those.*

Exercise: Surprises and Unexpected Twists

Describe the surprises and unexpected twists in the movie you have chosen.

Volume 2. Tips & Hints

Chapter 7. How To Develop A Great Comedy Plot

This chapter is a tribute to

a true master of comedy –

Charlie Chaplin

Comedy genre is very special and dear to the heart of every viewer, and it would be impossible to imagine the cinema without it, just like it would be impossible to live without laughter or positive emotions. When we go to see a comedy, we want to have fun, laugh heartily, experience light and happy feelings afterward.

But do we always get what we hope for from a comedy? Unfortunately, we do not. Many of us often leave the cinema thinking: "Couldn't they come up something funnier? I've just wasted my time ..." Humor is often so offensive, flat, dumb or vulgar that after watching a movie you just want to forget about it. The story itself does not grip you, the events are dull, and the characters do not pique our interest.

Based on the above, we can safely conclude that those who create comedies do not always know, understand and take into account the basics that make the foundation of a truly funny and exciting movie.

But those basics do exist, and if you are going to work in a comedy genre – you need to know them.

This chapter is the result of observations and analysis of the elements and techniques used in those comedies that won the viewers' hearts and brought money and fame to their creators.

Here you will find nine ways to captivate and amuse the viewer that will help you create a screenplay for a comedy that can become an instant classic, and year after year entertain millions of comedy fans. If you like how this sounds – let's start!

In comedy, as well as in other genres, our primary task is to captivate the viewer. Captivate and then make him laugh, not letting him become bored. To achieve that, it's essential to combine elements that create interest and make people laugh throughout the whole film.

How can we create interest? The protagonist's goal, danger, antagonist, adventure, legend, mystery – all these components of an exciting story are still relevant here, of course. Comedy is no exception. It has the same laws. This genre must capture and keep the viewer's attention from the first minute to the last. But here we enhance the exciting story with a whole lot of LAUGHTER.

How can we make the audience laugh? This is what this chapter is about.

First of all, let's note that **laughter occurs as a result of a person observing some situation or action and realizing that it is ILLOGICAL.**

Recall any funny situation and you will find something illogical there – that is, something that should not have happened in those circumstances, in that location or next to those people. For example, a guy is walking down the street, he sees a girl and can't look away, and the next thing we hear is "BOOM!" The guy is lying on the ground next to the lamppost, holding his head. And if the post also falls (God forbid, on the guy or the girl), then this will be another illogic and could be used in a very light, unserious movie.

So, here are the nine essential elements of the comedy genre. All of them are used to a greater or lesser degree in those films that we can definitely call classic comedies.

The foundation of each element is ILLOGIC.

Key Elements of the Comedy Genre

1. Acting Without Having All The Data

This means that comic situations can occur because the hero (or his opponent) started acting even though he missed or did not have some important data.

For example, somebody did not give the hero all the details, or the hero did not listen, or he simply forgot some of the information, and now he is pursuing his goal ... suddenly he starts having problems!

With a bit of imagination, we can come up with the following situations:

• The hero is sent to sort things out with a bully (whom he has not yet seen), and he turns out to be a crazy karate man.

• The heroine finds out about an amazing man (according to the description, it's the man of her dreams) who wants to meet her. However, she misses the fact that he is 90 years old.

Remember the movie *The Heartbreak Kid*, where a guy marries a perfect (or so it seems) girl who reveals her true colors only during their honeymoon and turns out to be a capricious psycho.

As you can see, if you omit the necessary information from any situation, it will inevitably result in illogic and laughter.

2. Deception

This subject has been thoroughly covered elsewhere, but it provides an endless supply of comic material. If you think of any decent comedy, it will definitely have some deception or pretense.

There are three types of deception:

a) **Hiding something.** This first type of deception is a "gold mine" for jokes. The character did something that he does not want others to know. For example, he made a big mistake while doing an important task, and then tries to correct his error before others notice it (*Mr. Bean*, the episode with the ruined picture). To create a chain of funny situations, one simply needs to make more and more mistakes so that the number of "sins" that must now be hidden increases.

b) **False goal.** This is another type of deception. The hero begins doing something he shouldn't be doing or starts going towards a wrong target.

c) **Wrong source of information.** When a character trusts someone who should not be trusted, he experiences confusion and problems. The scriptwriter can successfully use this situation to create a sitcom. Example, a wife receives a letter in the mail stating that her husband is cheating on her. She hires a friend of hers, who is a private detective, to follow her husband. Then it turns out that this unfortunate letter was sent to her by this very private detective in order to get some work. By the way, this is one of the main techniques to create the confidence game story.

3. Pretense

Pretending to be somebody else (especially if done ineptly) usually causes laughter. Having the hero's cover nearly blown will create a lot of excitement and interest in the viewer. A man who clumsily pretends to be a woman, a nerdy virgin pretending to be a macho man, a botanist pretending to be a gangster – this topic is an inexhaustible source of jokes, funny situations and storylines. For example, an African millionaire prince pretends to be a simple student in *Coming to America.*

Please note that the comedy with the use of pretense allows you to make the story truly exciting due to the threat of exposure constantly looming over the hero. "Will they uncover his identity now or will he manage to get out of it again?" This is the question that the viewer should be asking himself many times throughout the film. Be sure to build the plot in such a way that the protagonist is always on the verge of exposure. Make sure that he would get in big trouble if his pretense is discovered (a blow to his reputation, financial problems or even a death penalty). This is an excellent tool for combining the viewer's laughter and interest.

4. Unfamiliarity

If you send a person to an area that he is not familiar with, it can result in a lot of funny situations. This happens because the character is uninformed and incompetent in the new field. For example, the character may not know the laws and customs of the wild tribe where he suddenly finds himself; the heroine, who grew up surrounded by servants, may not know how to manage the household.

Remember that episode of the brilliant comedy *Some Like It Hot* when the main character invites Sugar to someone else's yacht having no idea what and where everything is. As a result of being unfamiliar with his surroundings, the hero has to find clever solutions for uncomfortable situations he gets himself into. The viewer laughs, and this episode will forever remain a classic of a comedy genre.

If you want to cultivate the ground for creating hilarious situations, put a character (or a group of characters) in the circumstances that are opposite to everything they are used to in life, to what they know and what they are able to do. And then quickly write down all the "illogics" that your creative imagination starts suggesting to you.

Examples: *Coming to America* (an African prince who had been surrounded by servants since childhood has to find his way in modern America); *Kate and Leopold* (a gentleman from the 19th century suddenly finds himself in present-day New York City).

5. Mix-Up

This is one of the main sitcom principles where the source of laughter is usually random coincidences, happenstance and the like. Based on one comic circumstance you can come up with a whole chain of funny situations.

When writing a comedy script, you can choose a specific situation and see what happens if some key character mixes up the correct sequence of actions, time or place of a meeting, etc. For example, our characters are the actors in a play. One of the actors is late and confuses the scenes. In a hurry, he jumps onto the stage with a dagger to kill his wife who at that moment should be in the arms of her lover. But there is no lover (this is the next scene) ... and now he must somehow get out of this mix-up.

6. Assumption

Sometimes in our life there are situations where we do not quite understand what's happening, and then our mind starts assuming things. If we start acting on such assumptions or someone's "authoritative" opinion instead of accurate, confirmed facts, the consequences can be either tragic or very comical. For example, in *Tropic Thunder,* a group of actors who are under the impression they are making a Vietnam war movie, wanders dangerously in the jungle and runs into a gang of real drug lords. Assuming everything is part of the film the actors empty-handedly start fights with the gang and get themselves into other comical situations along the way.

7. Inability

A great comedy technique — the protagonist takes on a task that he is not quite able to perform. An endless number of comedies are based on that principle.

In the comedy *See No Evil, Hear No Evil* a blind man and a deaf man run the operation of neutralizing criminals, and funny situations happen one after another. This comedy could have definitely been made more exciting, but the concept behind it is an inexhaustible source of comic situations.

Then we can look at the example of such movies as *Yes Man,* where the main character can only give affirmative answers, as well as *Liar, Liar*, where the hero cannot lie — two comedies that have become a classic thanks to masterfully used "inabilities."

It should also be noted here that the use of this comic element is a perfect opportunity to show the protagonist's personal growth. That is, starting with an inability, we end up with skills and ability. We get the desired change in the hero, which, in turn, causes emotional reaction in the audience.

8. Something That Should Not Be There

If a new husband is getting advice from his mother during his wedding night - what to do and how - while she is sitting near his bed, this would be a good example of "what should not be there." When someone or something is absolutely inappropriate for a particular situation, we get this comic element.

An action done at the wrong time and place (by mistake or carelessness) can lead to a funny situation. Similarly, an object placed in a location where it should not be present can cause a burst of laughter.

As an example of this point here is a real story that I came across online. Once upon a time, there was a family. The wife had been saving money to buy a beautiful chandelier, and finally she and her husband were able to buy it. They brought it home and the husband got up on a chair, took a huge glass chandelier in his hands and began wiring it. Meanwhile, the wife was standing nearby and helping out. At some point she got bored, apparently, and decided to play a little trick. She gave her husband a light flick (sorry for the juicy details) on the scrotum while he was working with the wires ... The husband jumped up in the air, dropped the chandelier and whispered with horror: "I got electrocuted down to my balls ..." In the end, the expensive chandelier was smashed to smithereens, and the husband never learned the truth.

9. Exaggerated Irrationality

This is a significant exaggeration of some non-optimal behavior. All the scriptwriter needs to do in this case is to take some peculiarity of the mind or an external feature of the character and increase it several times to make it look absurd and ridiculous. Thus, we can visualize the following irrationalities: a woman who is constantly cleaning because she thinks that there are deadly germs everywhere; a mother diligently educating her son, who is pushing sixty; a guy who wears sunglasses even in dark winter evenings thinking that it's "cool," and so on.

Imagine this character - a blonde who believes that she always (even at home) needs to wear high heels to be sexy.

This is an example of irrationality. A scriptwriter could send her on a walking tour on the sandy terrain with a heavy backpack. Of course, she would put on her high heels for this tour. This will be an exaggerated irrationality.

In the chapter "Character Development" there is a paragraph about developing characteristics (external and internal) of the character. If you are creating comic characters, those features have to be strengthened and exaggerated. An example of a comedy where several characters at once demonstrate such exaggerated irrationality would be the *Police Academy*.

We now have considered nine key points that form the foundation of an excellent comedy. Note that all these points have something in common – the illogic.

As already mentioned above, laughter results from the person's awareness or observation of some ILLOGIC in a situation or action. And this is the main secret of any comedy.

Deception, pretense, inability and other elements described above are your helpers in creating comic situations and truly funny stories. So now you have a tool for creating humor.

I wish you a lot of new ideas and look forward to seeing the screen versions of your brilliant comedies – the kind that can be watched again and again for many years, the kind where at the end we hear time and again, "What a wonderful, timeless classic!"

Chapter 8. What To Do If The Script Does Not Have Enough Tension

When you feel that there is "something wrong" with the script, most often it's the matter of tension, or rather, its absence.

Tension is an invisible thing, which is woven into the fabric of an exciting story like veins into the body. Without it, the box office figures are at zero. With it – we have lines at the movie theaters.

One of the first laws of film production is:

IF THERE IS NO TENSION IN THE SCRIPT - THE PRODUCER MAKES NO PROFIT.

To recognize the lack of tension in the script you just need to answer a few questions:

- Do you think that the story could have been made even more interesting?
- Do you feel that certain episodes are missing something, even though in general you consider your script worthy of screen adaptation?
- Does the storyline seem too plain and you want to make it more exciting?
- Your story has potential, but it does not seem to pique one's interest in its existing form?

If you answered "yes" to at least one of these questions then, most likely, the problem is in the lack of tension. That's easy to fix.

There are four methods to increase the tension in a script.

Method 1. Focus on the Protagonist's Goal

As you know, in any captivating story the main character has a goal that he follows throughout the script. In a well-designed story, obstacles and barriers do not break or stop the hero. He does not give up but seeks new ways to achieve his goal.

If there is not enough tension in the script, ask yourself two questions:

- Does the protagonist follow his goal throughout the WHOLE script?

- Does this goal stay as vital to him as the story unfolds, as it was at the beginning?

For example, the protagonist has a goal of becoming the world boxing champion. At the beginning of the story he trains a lot and pursues this goal. But one quarter into the script he happens to find himself on a desert island, and now he is busy hunting wild animals. The goal is lost. Even if he returns to boxing by the end of the story, we don't know that we will be able to keep the viewer's attention up to that point.

The rule is as follows: The goal of the protagonist must permeate all episodes of the script, regardless *of whether he gets closer to it or moves further away.*

Many scriptwriters make the mistake of breaking this rule. For example, they introduce a love story into the script, which, in itself, is fine, but it's not at all relevant to the main goal of the protagonist. As a result, the tension can noticeably decrease.

Method 2. Focus on the Main Conflict

Confrontation of forces should be maintained throughout the script. Examples of this: Titanic, Avatar, Terminator, etc.

Tension exists as long as there is a balance of opposing forces. As soon as one of the forces gets weaker, it becomes easy to predict future events and the tension immediately decreases.

For example, a guy meets a girl and they fall in love. They are planning to get married. However, another man gets in his way and steals the girl. The wedding is cancelled. The protagonist is depressed. There are now two options of what could happen next. The first one - the protagonist gives up, which means that no matter what we are going to reveal about his life now, the tension will be lost since the main conflict is no longer there. The second option - the protagonist is going to try to win his girlfriend back. Then the conflict stays intact, and the tension remains strong.

Both the protagonist and the antagonist should not only have a plan "B," but also plan "C," "D," "E" and the rest of the alphabet until they reach the climax.

And when the main conflict is ablaze, continue to throw the "firewood into the furnace." If this is a story about special forces vs. terrorists, then the tension is maintained by having continuous terrorist attacks. If we are writing about a romantic relationship, then have the heroine look at other men from time to time, for example.

Nothing should extinguish the hot line of the main conflict.

Method 3. Pressure of Time

If we want the script to have tension, the protagonist must act within a specific time frame. You should take into account that the time constraint can be created not only because the hero needs to be somewhere at a particular moment, but also because he is running out of oxygen, resources, etc.

Examples of time frames: the phone is discharging and makes it difficult to perform the task; the hero is running out of gasoline; a virus was injected into the body and there is a certain period of time to use the antidote; limited amount of food or water, the amount of air left in the tank while under water, and so on.

Does your main character have an interview for his dream job? Create tension not only during the scene of the interview itself. Make him sleep in that morning so that he is only a few seconds away from being unacceptably late.

Is your protagonist sailing on the ship to his destination? Make it so that the vessel could cross the narrow strait during the high tide only. And when the ship is almost out of danger, let the tide start falling, exposing the rocks. The crew members will have to hurry up to save the ship and their lives. You can add tension to almost any episode by using the time factor.

Method 4. Raise the Stakes

How dramatic are the consequences of the protagonist not reaching his goal and how much of that is shown in the script? How strong will be the pain of his loss?

It is very important to show what is at stake and demonstrate its value.

Is your character a forward on a soccer team? Show that all of his life he wanted his team to win the World Cup. Several times they were close to this goal but never achieved it. And now he is no longer a young man. This is his last chance to win as his football career is coming to an end. In other words - if not now, then never.

A guy saves his girlfriend from a drug dealer's slavery? Show how important the girl is to him. It is important to show that without her, his life has no meaning. This is what we mean by "the stakes." In this case, the tension is created not only by the chase scenes and showdowns but by demonstrating that the life of his girl is much more important to the protagonist than his own.

Make the events more dramatic through raising the stakes, and you will get extra tension in the story.

Using these four methods, you can increase the tension in any script and prepare it for screen adaptation.

Best of luck!

Chapter 9. How To Finalize Your Script

How many people that we've never heard of could have become successful scriptwriters? How many screenplay ideas did not break free onto paper and remained in the heads of those whose bodies now rest in peace in city cemeteries? However, the saddest thing is how many unfinished screenplays now gather dust inside the desk drawers (or are hidden somewhere among the computer files) of those who could never kick themselves hard enough and FINALIZE THE SCRIPTS THEY'VE STARTED.

Of course, there will always be a million reasons that prevent us from writing: our laziness, the wife, the children, mother-in-law and "I need to make money now" ... Or the husband, girlfriends, laundry, Internet and "how many times are you going to interrupt me?" One can always find lots of excuses as well as various household distractions.

However, what would you think if a protagonist of a new action flick suddenly stopped halfway to his goal about 30 minutes into the movie and said, "OK, I've had enough! Nothing seems to be going right." Then the screen would go dark, and the lights would come on. Completely confused, you would ask yourself, "Who made such a crappy movie?"

After all, my friend, our life is just as much of an action movie, even though we often do not see it as such. Perhaps in our dull daily battles for survival we simply forget that. What do our former classmates call it? The "daily grind."

Well, let us give them a tap on the shoulder and say, "What dreams and goals have you lost, buddy?" Yes, that's right. The daily grind is a state when there are no goals. Our eyes sparkle and energy abounds as long as we hear the patter

151

of hooves under us, as long there is the wind in our faces, and we keep pounding the keyboard.

Do you want to get your script done? Does it resist like crazy? Then, let's apply the black belt techniques from the professional screenwriter's manual. First, you should realize the following: it is not the screenplay that keeps resisting, it is SOMETHING inside of you. Therefore, your task is to conquer this SOMETHING or die in the battle. Do not settle for anything less than that.

Here is the first technique: SET A GOAL FOR YOURSELF: "I want to finish this script." Well, there is actually more to your goal than that. World champions always know a few little secrets, and in our case, this is something that is very often (more often than you think) overlooked when working on a script, and that is THE DEADLINE. I mean the exact date, by which you want to get the finished product! So if you stopped working, you need to restore your goal that includes the exact deadline (or set a new date) and keep creating your work!

The second technique: set the INTERMEDIATE GOALS all the way to the big victory. Each intermediate goal is a blow to that SOMETHING that is resisting inside of you. These smaller goals could be: to finish the episode plan, write the first ten pages, write the next ten pages and so on.

The third technique: be sure to create a SCHEDULE for your writing activities. If scriptwriting is your main work, you need to know when you start writing and how long you are going to continue writing, no matter what. For example, from 9 AM to 2 PM. Also, when you write, you WRITE! Feel free to send packing anyone who tries to disturb you. This is YOUR time. Sternly cock the trigger without taking your eyes off the monitor, point your Colt at the enemies of your schedule and ... keep writing.

The fourth techniques: eliminate any DISTRACTING factors. Here, the first step is to switch off all the phones. Yes, I mean switch them off. Do not turn the silent mode on, press the Switch Off button. Otherwise, on your way to the bathroom or while getting another cup of coffee you will have the urge to check who called you. Then your attention goes to the caller and you start wondering, "But what if it is something urgent?"

The next difficult step is to disconnect from the Internet according to your daily writing schedule. No such excuses as "I need the information," or "I have to switch my attention." While you are working, the Internet is a distracting factor and you should not compromise. If you need to search for some information online, just schedule a separate time for that process.

Just this last technique (switching off your phone and disconnecting from the Internet) will take you to unprecedented heights of scriptwriting performance.

Well, ladies and gentlemen, shall we recap?

We have our goal and our schedule, we do not allow any distracting factors to lead us astray, and we write as fast as we can. All doubts disappear when you just WRITE, so keep writing, no matter what.

If you stopped writing, force yourself to continue. Do not give up. Your hidden internal enemy is waiting for the first signs of weakness. Do not forget that your life is the most important screenplay, so make yourself proud. At first it will be difficult. Just sit down and write. Soon that SOMETHING that was restraining you will start giving in. Each touch of the keyboard will finish IT with a round of machine-gun fire until IT is unable to even crawl.

Well, cast a farewell glance over IT and keep writing. Continue to write until you make the insurance shot along with the last tap of your keyboard.

After that, you can lean back in your chair and wipe off the sweat from your forehead. Now you will be able to enjoy the incredible, glorious feeling that comes when you see the last six letters appear on the monitor one by one with each tap of your fingers: T-H-E E-N-D ...

Chapter 10. How to Improve The Scriptwriter's Performance

We use up a lot of energy when we write, so it's time to talk about how we can replenish our resources. We will also discuss the right way to work on the script so that your desire to continue writing never goes away.

Here are some symptoms of "writer's fatigue":

- a feeling of *physical* fatigue after computer work

- feeling "empty" as a result of working to meet the customer's deadline

- it makes you sick to look at your own workplace

- after your work on the script is interrupted, it is difficult to force yourself to get back into a creative mode

If you have never experienced that, this chapter is not for you. Do not waste your time. For those who have – there are some proven solutions.

I think you would agree that the problems listed above affect adversely any person who writes. After all, (attention!) in the work of the scriptwriter HE is the one who produces the "final product." That is, the scriptwriter's body and mind are his main equipment, however strange that may sound. In many respects, the quality of the finished script depends on the condition of this "equipment."

Not understanding this simple truth, many screenwriters make a big mistake of literally "burning" themselves with the work. If we wear out and don't service the "main equipment" in a timely fashion, we can get performance failures and undesirable disorders in the "mechanisms" of the body and mind. Consequently, the time gets wasted because those "defective" pages have to be deleted or rewritten afterwards anyway.

I think you understand this well and never give up; you do your best to survive while writing "the next episode" by yourself. Nevertheless, I am sure that the principles of improving the performance listed below will help you BUILD YOURSELF UP and achieve your goals.

Principles of Improving the Scriptwriter's Performance

1. Communicate with the area you are writing about.

It often happens that we need to write about something that we have never experienced before. For example, a screenwriter grew up in a big city. He has never seen a farm and doesn't know how to milk a cow. Then he gets hired to write a screenplay about the life of a family that lives on a farm in a remote village, where the farm life is a source of happy experiences as well as difficulties for them.

Perhaps, someone would say that you can simply read up online about this subject and that is enough ... However, this won't be very helpful. You can spend days doing that, but you still will not be able to write properly about this topic. To ACTIVELY create on a given subject, you must get a feel for it; you have to "become" one of those villagers (while working on the screenplay, of course). Therefore, the best way to write well about it and without further difficulties is for you to go ahead and visit a village, look at everything and feel it with your own hands, communicate with these people, and to UNDERSTAND that life.

2. Watch movies and read books.

You have certainly noticed that when you work in a particular genre, you can "tune in to the wavelength" by watching some movies in this genre. They make you burst with new ideas, and your imagination gets very creative.

As the work of a scriptwriter has a lot to do with intellectual labor and creating "thought forms" (which often is even more exhausting than physical work), it is important that you receive something SIMILAR in exchange.

Watching movies and reading books allows to "feed the screenwriter's mind." That way you can keep the balance and won't experience any "imagination deficiency."

3. Eat well and take vitamins.

This is an elementary rule directly related to mental activity. If you are not eating regularly or your diet is inadequate, it will affect the condition of your body and its ability to produce energy. When there is not enough energy, it is going to be difficult to put on paper what you have conceived in your mind.

Vitamins will allow you to save and accumulate the necessary energy. If you try taking them for some time and then stop – you will see a huge difference. Do not skimp on this.

4. Get enough sleep.

Sleep is the main way for your body to recover. If you neglect it in the name of creativity, sooner or later it will take a toll on you and your creativity. And it will hurt. You know exactly how much sleep your body needs, therefore, try to sleep at least as much. You will have more physical and mental endurance, you will be more productive and quick-witted.

5. Do not take painkillers.

Recent studies show that in addition to the destructive effect of painkillers on the person's internal organs, they also dull perceptions, analytical activity and ability to think clearly. If you look at the side effect warning for these drugs, you will see many contraindications such as driving restrictions, recommendations not to do anything that requires attention or focus, and so on. These drugs can give a "momentary feeling of clarity," however shortly after you will experience the dullness and weakening of all senses; more importantly — drugs do block mental processes.

6. Do not overindulge in alcohol.

You may have heard such phrases as "But it helps me be more creative! It makes my imagination better ..." or "I need to be a little crazy to write something brilliant, so every day before starting my work I have a drink." It does not matter how you justify it. This approach will never lead to sustainable success. Alcohol significantly reduces your ability to think and express your ideas in writing; your reactions slow down as well. Of course, this is a personal matter. However, remember that the product you create has a direct impact on the society and the culture of the whole country or even several countries, so you must ensure that your product is really high-quality.

We all know those screenplays that were written with a "daily joint," and they do not actually bring any profits to their producers or benefit our society.

7. Get sufficient rest.

Sometimes in an attempt to make a decent income, you can forget about quality rest. What is quality rest? It can be whatever lets you take your attention off your writing, switch it to something else and makes you feel that you can temporarily forget about your work. It can be a two-day fishing trip or a couple of hours of tennis, a day off in the country, some gardening or a mini-trip.

What's important is that after resting you feel you have a fresh outlook on your workplace and your work goes easier and faster.

Remember the feeling when you came back home from a two-week vacation? I think you would agree that you looked differently at everything. It is important to learn how you can fundamentally switch your activity for a short period of time. I am sure you will be able to find affordable and effective options for such weekly breaks.

8. Take walks in the open air.

Do you remember how you feel at the end of a productive day of writing when you are a little "not there" or feel that "it's hard to focus"?

In those moments it is very helpful to take a walk. After you are done working, try to go outside instead of escaping to the online world as it can make you feel even "foggier."

When you walk – look around, watch people, cars, and nature. It is a good way to "pull out" stuck attention from inside of your head; you can "come back to life" and recover quickly. Try and take your time doing it!

9. Exercise.

You actually perform a lot of mental work. After such work there is a feeling that the body is tired as well. However, it is not factually so. On the contrary, the body demands energy and the energy comes from motion. When you exercise the body is receives oxygen, becomes fit, it gets energetic and enables you to work even more actively.

In addition to keeping you healthy and preventing various unwanted conditions from a sedentary lifestyle, exercising helps create high morale and improve strength and endurance.

10. Do not start working in a bad mood.

There are times when someone or something can upset us. In those moments the negative emotions prevail over the positive, and if need to write about something other than "taking revenge on someone," it is better not to start your work at this time. Wait a little bit, take a walk, and when you feel that things have calmed down - get to work. Otherwise you will bring negative emotions into your creation, and in most cases, you'll need to rewrite it later anyway.

11. Do not tolerate (do not agree with) distractions.

In the chapter "HOW TO FINALIZE YOUR SCRIPT" we have already touched upon this subject. However, let us consider again what could be such a distracting factor. When you are focused on the script, something (or someone) can interrupt or distract you. For example, somebody can ask you what you wrote so far, or meow loudly because you forgot to feed it ... All these things are distractions, and they slow you down or even sidetrack you from the main goal – writing a planned number of pages. Therefore, do your best to remove them from your life as an author.

12. Gain momentum.

I think you have experienced this many times: when you start writing again after a break, at first you may feel as if you are pushing up against something incredibly heavy. The solution is to CONTINUE pushing against this "heavy thing."

Imagine that you need to start a locomotive. How easy would it be to get it moving with a massive load behind it? Could this locomotive move immediately at the maximum speed? No. It needs to gain momentum.

Now imagine that you have got it up to speed. It's now going as fast as you need, and all you have to do is to keep it up. You don't have to "push this heavy thing" anymore.

It is the same with writing: it is important to accelerate and maintain it at the highest possible speed.

Nevertheless, if you happened to stop for some reason, perhaps, you will need to break through that "invisible wall," accelerate yourself again in order to reach the speed you had before stopping. Of course, it is better to simply prevent the stops. To ensure that, it is necessary to implement all the points described above.

13. Do not deviate from the goals you set.

Perhaps, sometimes you can find yourself in the following situation: you start working on a promising project, then suddenly other promising projects come up or, perhaps, something is tempting you to quit the one you had started originally. Those offers may not even be related to writing scripts whatsoever; however, they are very "promising." Of course, you should be flexible here and consider and analyze all offers and existing projects. However, take into account that life can sidetrack you. And that is one of the traps in any activity.

Your successes and victories are directly related to your ability to complete what you have started. No matter what may get in your way or whatever doubts may arise, despite the well-wishers advising you to "give it up and do something more profitable," or saying that "this is not popular right now, so you should write about the ...." Write until you complete what you started. Be sure to finish writing the script; do not leave the work half done.

Consider new offers only after completing the work. Otherwise, you can make a mistake. After all, it is quite possible that the "unfinished screenplay" that will take only two more weeks of work is the key to your dreams. Who knows?

In the future, if you feel any symptoms of "writer's fatigue" – just look through this chapter, apply the appropriate recommendations, get rehabilitated and take your script to the finishing line.

Better yet — from the very beginning create a "safety margin" by applying the above principles on a regular basis. That way you will be able to devote yourself to your favorite work as much as you wish.

Epilogue

So, we have come to the end. Let's recap.

We've learned how to start working on any script or book, how to structure a story, how to develop characters, how to make the plot truly exciting, and even how to write a comedy.

We've learned that a well-developed plot makes for a great screenplay or book, while a weak one will probably never get finished.

As you may have noticed, this manual describes a step-by-step process. Following these steps, you can move from the initial ideas to a completed, interesting and exciting plot. A lot of things happen during this process that let your imagination fly high and enable you to create the work on the level you desire.

Think of this manual as a tool that will help you, the author, realize your wildest creative ideas. Use this tool, go from one step to the other and record everything you develop.

It was an honor for me to introduce this step-by-step technology to you because I know that you are one of those people who is changing the world and creating a better future.

My sincere wish for you is that your already powerful imagination becomes even stronger, and you begin using your full potential. I believe that at the heart of any culture are two things: works of art and productivity. I know a lot of people who write well, but after one screenplay or one book, they don't continue writing. Either their imagination runs out of new ideas, or they do not have enough self-confidence. I want you to not just create works of art, but to be super productive in that. I want you to be able to CREATE a LOT so that nothing could stop you. I know that many of you can rise very high with your art and raise this world along with you. But you and I will have to work on that.

In the end, I'd like to give you some advice.

First, always remember: there is nothing more valuable than your own point of view. When you lose your point of view – you lose your project, your way and your dreams. When you work on a project, a screenplay or a book, when you create characters or a whole fictional world, do not let anyone interfere and ruin it. The best answer to the critic's attacks is the following: "OK, I understand your point of view. What are your suggestions?" This question will scare the critics away once and for all, and you will be able to continue creating your own universe in peace. A constructive person, however, will actually give you some suggestions, and then you will decide for yourself whether to accept them or not.

Second, never underestimate your potential. Create your own stories as if you were Quentin Tarantino or Luc Besson. By that I mean create with the confidence that if you write something, it will be seen by millions. The worst enemy of imagination is the lack of confidence in your abilities.

Never underestimate your own potential. If you believe in your dream, then life itself will give you the chance to make it a reality.

And may everything go your way!

Keep in touch.

Alexander Astremsky

STORY FLASH

WORKBOOK

FOR CREATING STORIES AND CHARACTERS

THIS IS A TOOL THAT WILL HELP YOU
CREATE MORE

THIS IS A BRIDGE BETWEEN YOUR
IDEA AND THE FINISHED BOOK

THIS IS A MAP TO YOUR ADVENTURE
IN CREATING A NEW LITERARY WORK

About The Story-Flash Workbook

The *Story-Flash* WORKBOOK (*Story-Flash System Book 2*) is an excellent companion for this book.

The workbook is meant to be used to develop the screenplays "on paper," not in front of the screen. Take it with you to the park, on a business trip, use it on the plane or at the beach. It is also perfect for those times when you are tired from constantly looking at the screen.

The workbook will enable you to develop the plot with the help of the exact technology without having to consult this book every time. To use it, simply write down the IDEA and then build up your story from there, step-by-step. From the moment you wrote down the primary situation and created the protagonist and antagonist, you can move forward without any stops until your story is built from A to Z.

The first section of the workbook allows you to create the nucleus that you will use to build the plot. The second section helps you build the structure. By doing the steps of the third section you will develop memorable and three-dimensional characters. And the fourth section will help you add tension to the story so that the readers (or viewers) cannot tear themselves away from it.

By the way, I think it's a good idea to have as many such workbooks as you have ideas in your head! That way you can easily make each of them into a finished story!

25 Reasons to Use the Workbook

1. With this Workbook, you can transfer all your ideas onto paper step by step.

2. This is a proven approach to the plot development.

3. You will not be distracted by messengers and social networks.

4. You can work on several Workbooks simultaneously and develop several stories at once.

5. The Workbook will not let a single idea of yours fall through the cracks.

6. You immediately know which section to use to write down your ideas.

7. You can take it with you to the park, on a business trip, use it on an airplane or at the beach.

8. It includes all the steps of the Story-Flash technology described in this book.

9. The Workbook will be your guide in developing the story and its characters.

10. It will be helpful to those who are new to screenwriting (or writing) as well as to professionals.

11. This is the best way to focus on the task of developing a story.

12. It is perfect for use when you are away from your computer or tired of constantly looking at the screen.

13. You can always keep it handy.

14. It is great for children or teenagers who want to write stories or books, but do not know where to start.

15. You will always be ready for a flash of inspiration.

16. *This Workbook will help you develop the plot quicker than you've ever imagined.*

17. *Writer's block becomes a thing of the past because now you always know what the next step is in the development of your story.*

18. *You will forget what it means to have no inspiration.*

19. *This is your partner in the plot development. Together you can make the story so profound and multifaceted that it would be possible to write a script or a novel based on it.*

20. *You will completely eliminate the confusion in your head.*

21. *You can transfer all your ideas onto paper and get a clear structure for your plot.*

22. *You will have a strong plot with no "holes" or "inconsistencies."*

23. *The Workbook is going to save you from weeks of "the throes of writing."*

24. *It will save your precious time.*

25. *It will let you use your imagination to the fullest extent!*

All the steps in the *Story-Flash* system reinforce and complement each other. Follow it page by page, write line after line, and very soon you will have a finished story!

Dear reader!

Did you receive value from STORY-FLASH? Please you leave an Amazon review and share your feedback. This will help future readers choose the book and get benefits just like you did.

Thank you!

If you would like to receive the updates from the STORY-FLASH project and the STORY-FLASH Magazine, please subscribe here http://story-flash.com/Subscription

Let's work together! I am always happy to work with you.
If you need help with developing your plot, writing a screenplay, or if you would like to organize a STORY-FLASH workshop or game for your audience, please contact me at
info@story-flash.com

STORY-FLASH.COM

Made in the USA
Lexington, KY
08 March 2019